DRAIN THE SWAMP

Drain the Swamp

HOW WASHINGTON CORRUPTION IS WORSE THAN YOU THINK

Congressman **Ken Buck**
with Bill Blankschaen

REGNERY
PUBLISHING
A Division of Salem Media Group

Published in association with the literary agency of Legacy, LLC, 501 N. Orlando Avenue, Suite #313-348, Winter Park, FL 32789.

Regnery® is a registered trademark of Salem Communications Holding Corporation

Cataloging-in-Publication data on file with the Library of Congress

ISBN 978-1-62157-638-9

Published in the United States by
Regnery Publishing
A Salem Communications Company
300 New Jersey Ave NW
Washington, DC 20001
www.Regnery.com

Distributed to the trade by
Perseus Distribution
www.perseusdistribution.com

Manufactured in the United States of America

10 9 8 7 6 5 4 3 2 1

Books are available in quantity for promotional or premium use. For information on discounts and terms, please visit our website: www.Regnery.com.

CONTENTS

PREFACE

"Government is like a baby. An alimentary canal with a big appetite at one end and no sense of responsibility at the other."

—Ronald Reagan

O n November 1, 2016, my daughter gave me the greatest gift a dad could ever dream of—my first grandchild, Barrett "Bear" Schwartz. While serving my initial term in Congress, I shared many of the same characteristics that Barrett had when he came into this world. We were both stunned by our new surroundings, and unable to communicate with those around us about the gravity of our concerns.

Luckily for Bear, he has two great parents and he received the attention he needed at birth. I have been less fortunate in trying to work with my colleagues to fix the mess in Congress. My answer is to write this book to speak directly to the American people and try to work with them outside the beltway to drain the Washington swamp.

Bear and I also share similar financial burdens. My mortgage approximates Bear's share of the national debt. However, my mortgage helped me live in a comfortable home. Bear has nothing substantial to show for the debt he acquired at birth. It was passed on to him without his consent, a legacy of irresponsible decisions resulting from selfish, narcissistic behavior in Washington. His generation will live in a weaker America, a country that begs foreign nations and multinational corporations to finance our unquenchable desire to live beyond our means.

Democrats *and* Republicans, conservatives *and* liberals caused this financial disaster—the biggest disaster we face: our gargantuan national debt. Our elected officials, acting in concert, have deceived us into becoming complacent while plunging us further into bipartisan bankruptcy. Washington doesn't represent the American people anymore, because the bureaucrats and elected officials in Washington pursue their own self-serving agendas rather than doing what is objectively right for the country. The time for complacency about our federal government is long past. We Americans must exercise our constitutional rights to come together and make vital decisions to save our republic.

I dedicate this book to Bear and his generation who will, unfortunately, pay for Washington's corruption, its moral and financial bankruptcy. They will pay with lost opportunity, higher taxes, and a lower standard of living. I pray that Americans will revive the founders' spirit and take back our country—for Bear, for his generation, and for the future of the United States of America, the "last best hope of earth."

FOREWORD

BY FORMER SENATOR JIM DEMINT

I n the early days of our Republic, our nation's capital was an actual swamp.

Far from being an international symbol of freedom and prosperity, malaria-plagued Washington was considered a hardship assignment for European diplomats. The palaces of London, Paris, and Vienna were a world away from our humble White House and humid little Capitol buildings, with shantytowns for all the construction workers scattered in-between. Even our own presidents and congressmen didn't like coming here.

I sometimes think we'd be better off if the same were true today.

Most candidates for Congress talk incessantly about all the problems in Washington. Both Republicans and Democrats on the campaign trail rage about the big special interests driving the other party to take advantage of the poor, the children, the disabled, the young, the old, minorities, and all the forgotten Americans. Many talk about government waste, corruption, and unsustainable debt. Every candidate promises to fight for change. They all campaign as bold stallions. Why do most of them, once elected, serve as geldings?

Something happens to almost everyone who is elected to the U.S. House or the Senate. They all promise to charge into Washington and "drain the swamp." But it only takes a few months before they discover the swamp can be a pleasant hot tub. And they want to stay in for a nice long soak.

I remember as a freshman congressman sitting in one of our regular Wednesday morning Republican Conference meetings. There were about 200 Republicans in rows of folding chairs in front of the leadership table. The members were expected to listen respectfully to the presentations by our leadership team and then line up behind microphones in the aisles to ask questions. This meeting was like all the others I had experienced in my first two years. The leadership explained that we needed to vote for more bad bills or the Senate would pass something even worse, they promised to address the excessive spending and debt after the next election, and they admonished us all to raise more money to make sure we stayed in the majority.

I couldn't take it anymore. This was not why I left my business and spent weeks away from my family. Without thinking, I stood up and yelled, "This is completely irrational!" A deafening silence fell on the room as I considered the gravity of a freshman shouting down the Speaker of the House. I stood in the midst of this awkward silence facing the stares from the leadership table until someone in the back of the room mercifully shouted, "Don't worry, you'll get used to it!" I never did.

Congressmen like Ken Buck, who actually try to keep their campaign promises, do not find a welcome mat in Washington. I know because as both a congressman and senator, I found the D.C .Swamp is programmed to destroy anyone who tries to disturb the status quo. There really are big special interests that guard their nests like vultures. The big union bosses for government workers will spend millions to defeat anyone who dares to cut government spending or eliminate a wasteful government program. Big corporations will fight tooth and nail to protect their tax loopholes, credits, and targeted tariff waivers. All the big hospitals, banks, corporations, and media moguls actually push for more complex regulations because it gives them an advantage over their smaller competitors. Washington, D.C. *is* a swamp of murky water filled with terrapins, alligators, and venomous snakes, only we call them lobbyists, congressmen, and bureaucrats.

The American people deserve better, and all able-bodied citizens can help our representatives drain this swamp. Electing people with integrity and courage is part of the solution. But they can't drain the swamp without a lot of help from the American people. I've seen many good candidates prevail against all odds to become congressmen and senators. But I've also seen the pressures—and the pleasures —of Washington transform many of them into servants to the Washington Establishment: party leaders, lobbyists, and the media. All the pressures inside Washington are designed to keep the gravy train moving with more spending and more government control. Centralized government power always gives advantages to the big players in Washington, big players who usually don't have your best interests in mind.

Informed and active Americans can change Washington. But we have to understand *what* is actually happening inside the Washington beltway and *why* it is happening. Ken Buck's *Drain the Swamp* is a critically important book because it will help the reader experience the swamp through the eyes of a new congressman. It will help you understand why most congressmen and senators "drink the Kool-Aid," and forget all their campaign promises.

The American people can become the counterbalance to the big special interest pressure groups that inhabit Washington. But Americans must first know the truth about what is actually happening inside the Capitol. You will *not* learn the truth from the mainstream media. Even some "right-of-center" media outlets have painted a skewed picture of the courageous and principled members of Congress like Ken Buck and the House Freedom Caucus and Senate Steering Committee.

You *will* learn the truth from *Drain the Swamp* and find out how American citizens can elect and support congressmen and senators who will keep their oath to defend the Constitution and will serve the best interests of the American people.

Let's stand together and pull the plug on the swamp! If not you, who? If not now, when?

Jim DeMint
President, The Heritage Foundation

CHAPTER 1

WHY WASHINGTON IS A SWAMP

"The hottest places in hell are reserved for those who in times of moral crises preserve their neutrality."[1]

—President John F. Kennedy

There are three types of lies, according to Mark Twain: lies, damn lies, and statistics. After I served in the U.S. House of Representatives for only two months, I discovered a fourth type of lie, perhaps the biggest ever told—*House budgets.*

As a first term congressman, I was excited to read the House Budget Committee's 2015 plan for balancing the budget in ten years. What I found alarmed me; it was all make-believe: projections without plans, assumptions that were in some cases contradictory. The budget claimed savings from repealing Obamacare (still a wish rather than a reality), while simultaneously counting Obamacare taxes as ongoing revenue. The budget plan magically cut food stamps and welfare by $1 trillion without a plan do so and tossed in $147 billion in assumed "dynamic" economic growth for good measure.

After reading this fiction disguised as a budget, I told a reporter, "I don't know anyone who believes we're going to balance the budget in ten years. It's all hooey." One member of the budget committee had the gall to say of this fantasy plan that "a budget is a moral document; it talks about where your values are." All I can say is that lies, damn lies, and imaginary statistics don't represent my values.

A member of the Republican Whip asked if I was a *yes* or *no* vote on the budget; I told him I was neither. I was a *hell no*!

"But why?" he asked. "The budget balances in ten years."

I asked him how long he had been in Congress.

"Fourteen years."

"Did they tell you ten years ago, that the budget would balance in ten years?"

He sighed. "You're right, this budget will never balance."

It's bad enough that the budget plan was designed to deceive the American people. Even worse was that House leadership handed us talking points to explain to our constituents how all these lies, damn lies, and false statistics balanced the budget, as if they did.

Washington is a swamp because Congress (and the Washington bureaucracy) wants it to be; and most Americans have been badly misinformed about why Washington doesn't work for them. It has nothing to do with gridlock or partisanship or political bickering. One of my first revelations when I became a congressman was how *non-adversarial* the atmosphere was. There was plenty of bipartisan agreement that Washington should increase the size of the federal government and spend money it doesn't have. Members of Congress are, for the most part, fat and happy alligators who feel pretty darned comfortable in the swamp of Washington.

WASHINGTON VALUES VS. AMERICAN VALUES

And there's the problem. Most of us didn't grow up thinking about politics or economics the way they do in Washington. I certainly learned a different set of values from my grandfather, who opened a shoe repair store in Greeley, Colorado, in the 1930s.

My parents, who grew up during the Great Depression, and my grandparents taught me the value of hard work. My mom was the daughter of Norwegian immigrants who arrived in New York City as teens with nothing but a few dollars between them. She grew up in New York City while my dad grew up in Greeley, Colorado, not far from where I live now.

My parents had a very simple philosophy for me when I was a teen—either play sports or get to work. So I did both. I lettered in five different sports, and even managed to play football for four years while I attended Princeton University.

And because I wanted spending money, I worked too, and learned about the respect and responsibility that comes from hard work. I worked, variously, as a janitor—stripping and re-waxing floors, scraping gum off desks, and cleaning toilets—as a furniture hauler, as a truck driver on moving vans, and then as a crew foreman.

My favorite job by far was working on my aunt and uncle's ranch in Wyoming, which I started doing when I was twelve. I spent most summers there and learned to stack hay with a stacker—and then to re-stack it by hand when I messed up. One day I would be on a horse moving cattle, and the next day I'd be on a truck driving silage from the field to the silage pit.

I loved working at the ranch because it was such a peaceful atmosphere, and we solved problems. We had to. If we didn't do it, no one else would. No one on the ranch looked to Washington to fix broken fences. If a neighbor had a problem, another neighbor helped fix the problem. People came together to help one another with everything from helping a child get an education to helping a family in need of food or clothing.

It was, and still is, a community with very little government and a whole lot of neighborly interaction. It made a lasting impression on me, especially as I began my career in the world of politics after graduating from college.

I worked in the Wyoming state legislature, eventually got my law degree, and became an Assistant U.S. Attorney. It was then, as a prosecutor employed by the federal Department of Justice, that I saw how things took longer and costed more when Washington was involved. And I learned that results are often secondary to political concerns.

After stepping away from government for a period in private business, I re-entered politics, this time as the district attorney for Weld County, Colorado. Over my three terms, the adult crime rate decreased by 50 percent and we worked aggressively to deter and prevent juvenile crime. We got things done.

That's how America works, at least at the local level. We see a problem and we work together to solve it.

But in Washington that's not how it works at all. Members of Congress have only one problem that they're serious about solving—and that's getting reelected. And they're convinced that the path to reelection lies through bribing the American people with endless government programs we can't afford. That's not my agenda at all.

MOTIVATED TO MAKE A DIFFERENCE

When I decided to run for Congress, I was motivated to make a difference. In early 2013 I was diagnosed with cancer, non-Hodgkin's lymphoma, stage four. I had twenty-two tumors in my neck and twelve under my arm with cancer on my spleen and eight different bones in my body. Doctors told me that if I didn't have chemotherapy immediately I would be dead in three months; and even with immediate chemotherapy I had only a 50 percent chance of surviving.

But after two months of aggressive chemotherapy, another PET scan showed the cancer to be fully in remission. My doctors said my speedy recovery surprised and amazed them. To me, it was nothing less than a miracle from God. My last chemo session was on July 5, 2013. I called it my own Independence Day.

The entire ordeal reminded me that life is precious and time is short. I decided to run for Congress to see what good I could do with the time I had.

I didn't go to Congress to make a career, because I realized I could be dead tomorrow. I do believe that God made me for a purpose, and while I don't know how many terms I will serve in Congress, I do know that I want to use my time there to help solve the nation's problems. I want to get things done. But I have discovered that in Washington politicians define "getting things done" as looking out for their own interests, not yours, and I've become convinced that while we need principled leadership in Congress—lots of it—Congress will never reform itself because congressmen believe that reform is against their self-interests.

BIPARTISAN BANKRUPTCY

When I first arrived in Washington as a congressman in 2015, we had a Democratic president and a Republican-controlled House and Senate. I had enough political experience to consider myself a political realist, but even I was surprised at how aggressively Congress avoids solving problems.

I expected gridlock; instead, I found Democrats and Republicans cooperating to bankrupt the country by avoiding tough budget choices. America is going broke—fast. There are no two ways about it. We now exceed a mind-numbing $20 trillion in debt and we're going deeper into debt every day. Just in the time it took to read this sentence, America will be on the hook for another $65,000! Yet members of both parties continue to crank out federal budgets full of waste, with hundreds of billions of dollars in unauthorized expenditures—all the while telling America they've done the best they could do to preserve the freedoms we all hold dear.

In fact, they are undermining our freedoms every day. They undermine them with job-killing regulations and bureaucracy. And they undermine them by enslaving us and our children and our grandchildren with a heavy manacle of debt that threatens to destroy our economy.

Admiral Michael Mullen, a former chairman of the Joint Chiefs of Staff, said that the single greatest security threat we face—the one that keeps him awake at night—is not China, Russia, North Korea, or even Iran. It is our national debt.[2] He added, "We just can't be the country that we're capable of…if we keep spending ourselves into oblivion. We won't be able to make the investments [we need]."[3] He's right. Payments on the debt are already crowding out other priorities in our federal budget, including defense and infrastructure spending; and Congress has no realistic strategy—yet—to solve this problem. On the contrary, those in Congress have been content to make it worse, expanding that debt balloon as far as they can, because they think it wins votes and guarantees their power.

A CULTURE OF CORRUPTION

Money rules in Washington.

Most Americans don't realize that influence in Congress comes with a price tag. Members are required to pay for committee assignments. Chairmen are required to pay for their chairmanships. The Speaker, Leader, and Whip compete for the leadership position and then must pay millions of dollars for the honor of holding the office. Lobbyists, corporations, and wealthy individuals who need something from Congress raise the money.

For Republicans, all the money raised by these charges goes to the National Republican Congressional Committee (NRCC), supposedly to help get members elected. The reality is that NRCC funds are used to coerce members to vote with the leadership. When members don't vote the "right way," the funding dries up from the donor class, members are pressured to step down from their committee assignments, and the NRCC refuses to help finance their campaigns. I'll reveal more about the pay-to-play system in chapter three.

For now the important thing to know is that the result of this system is that members routinely vote for defective legislation in order to please party leaders and get money for their reelection campaigns instead of doing what is right for America. Congressional leadership, lobbyists, and outside interest groups collaborate to make the game work. They direct decision-making in what used to be known as the People's House.

By playing the game, these elected men and women who swore to uphold the Constitution from all enemies, foreign and domestic, trade the long-term security of our children and grandchildren for short-term political favors. That trade doesn't only lead to financial bankruptcy; it is also morally bankrupt.

I am a Republican, but the moment we put party over principle, we've lost. Both major political parties are guilty on this one. That's why I call the problem we face today *bipartisan bankruptcy*. Both parties have no problem letting the debt rise if that means they can avoid taking tough stands or making difficult decisions.

Barney Frank, the former Democratic congressman from Massachusetts with whom I agree on very little, was correct when he said: "This notion that members of Congress are power-hungry—absolutely the opposite. Most members like to duck tough issues." Exactly right. While some do pursue power and riches, most prefer to keep their heads down, look out for their own interests, and maintain the status quo—even if that means ignoring problems like our out-of-control national debt. Everyone uses government to get what he or she wants. And if that happens, our nation has no hope of a freedom-filled future.

A BIPARTISAN PROBLEM

It is true that former President Obama was a calamity when it came to our exploding national debt. But there's plenty of blame to go around. Congress is supposed to have the power of the purse, and yet the federal debt rose when the Democrats controlled Congress and it rose when Republicans controlled Congress. It is a bipartisan problem. We now owe more than $20 trillion in 2017—and that isn't even counting the unfunded liabilities we owe through programs like Social Security and Medicare. When we factor those numbers in, conservative estimates put our actual debt at more than $90.6 trillion. My friend Congressman David Brat, a former economics professor, estimates we will be facing $127 trillion in unfunded liabilities alone a mere ten years from now.[4]

Meanwhile, our political leaders always seem to have an excuse. When Republicans reclaimed the House in 2010 with a record-setting wave of new inductees, debt levels continued to rise. Republican leaders told voters they needed control of the Senate to make a difference. In 2014, voters gave them the Senate, and the House experienced another massive influx of Republican representatives.[5] Yet still the precipitous slide into bankruptcy has continued.

Can Trump make a difference? We'll see. The problems before us are massive, and President Trump has his own spending priorities, but at least the new administration has a commitment to action and acknowledges, as surprisingly few have done, that the national debt is one of the serious problems it has to tackle.

WHY I FIGHT

My message is not popular with the privileged in Washington and in the halls of Congress. I've had to face the fact that I will never be liked by those who want to maintain the status quo.

I checked into a Dallas hotel one evening and rushed to get in a workout. I was running on a treadmill next to another fellow who was watching television on his monitor. As we ran, I saw my picture appear on his monitor with a caption that read, "Worst Person in America," though I couldn't hear what was being said. The man looked over at me, looked at the monitor again, and then scowled back in my direction. Then he shook his head, ripped his earphones out and stormed out of the gym. I prayed silently, Lord, there are people who hate me when I speak the truth. And the words of the Truth-teller from Nazareth came to mind: "If the world hates you, keep in mind that it hated me first."

I believe the stakes are too high to remain silent. If we do not demand change now, America and all we love about her will be lost— and our children and grandchildren will know nothing but the very burdens from which our founders freed us just a few centuries ago.

Anyone who reads history knows how civilizations collapse:

- **They spend too much.** Budget crises have always been early warning signs of the collapse of an empire or a regime, and the bigger the government, the harder it falls.
- **Their people stop producing.** Civilizations grow when their people are hard-working, self-sacrificing, and entrepreneurial—and they collapse when they become lazy and self-centered and dependent on the state.
- **They become corrupt.** As the power of the state grows, so does official corruption, which the people are expected to overlook (or practice themselves on a smaller level).
- **They lose their *why*.** Eventually, civilizations lose sight of *why* they came to exist in the first place—their identity, their purpose. When a nation loses its sense of shared identity, the end is near, because no one is all that interested in fighting or sacrificing for a cause or an identity long forgotten.

I, for one, do not believe we have completely forgotten who we are as Americans, but I do believe that our Republic is in grave danger. Donald Trump was elected president to drain the Washington swamp. There is no national problem more pressing than that, because that problem touches virtually every other problem we face. This is our time, our opportunity to choose freedom over bondage and noble sacrifice that will help secure America's liberty over ignoble selfishness that will surely forfeit it. America's future is at stake. We need to drain the swamp in Washington, and we need to do it now.

PROTECTING AMERICA FROM THE GOVERNMENT

In this book, I will reveal what really goes on behind closed doors in Congress. It's not pretty, to be sure—and it's worse than you think.

The stories I will share will both shock and alarm you. But it is not a lost cause. I will also propose solutions for making Congress care about what is best for America—and you—once again. The solutions are not far-fetched and have already been proven to work when attempted. But they involve getting power out of the hands of those in Washington and returning it to the American people. Thomas Paine is widely attributed as saying, "It is the duty of the Patriot to protect his country from his government." We are charged with such a duty now.

CHAPTER 2

WELCOME TO WASHINGTON, CONGRESSMAN!

"Congress is so strange; a man gets up to speak and says nothing, nobody listens, and then everybody disagrees."

—Will Rogers

I felt as if I had won the lottery.

I entered the suite that had been prepared for me, as a newly elected congressman, at the Capitol Hill Hotel.

Inside my room I discovered a smorgasbord of gifts: a plush blanket with the congressional seal and Majority Leader Kevin McCarthy's signature; rich chocolates and assorted fine candies courtesy of Steve Scalise (Republican Whip), Cathy McMorris Rodgers (chair of the House Republican Conference), and other Republican leaders. I was impressed but also wondered who was paying for it.

On the campaign trail I had to live on fast food as I was driving from event to event. As a newly elected congressman, I was invited to countless Washington parties, where the dining was a good deal fancier.

The message that was hammered home over the eight days of orientation for new Republicans in Congress was: You have arrived. You are part of the club. And don't you forget it.

LET THE PARTIES BEGIN

When I asked why orientation lasted eight days (it seemed like it could be done much faster), I was told that it took eight days to fit in all the parties that the leadership wanted to host. Parties weren't add-ons to orientation; they were a big part of the point. Party leaders wanted to secure our support for their reelection to leadership and they wanted to make clear that if we were willing to play the Washington game, the party—the privileges and perks—could be ours forever.

As I joined the other new members that first day at the Capitol Hill Hotel, I'm sure many of us felt like we had arrived at high school for the first time. We were all a little nervous as we mingled, met, and acted as if we knew more than we did. But on the very first day, the free stuff started to flow.

Did we want a new iPhone or laptop? No problem. Any technology we could think of was available, and it wouldn't cost us anything—not really. We soon discovered that each member has a Member's Representational Allowance (MRA) to cover these costs as well as the cost of hiring staff and paying rent. So if we wanted an iPhone, it would just come out of our MRA. If we wanted a laptop, it came out of our MRA.

It wasn't like on the campaign trail where I had to dial for dollars and try to make the most of every penny given. If someone gave to my campaign, that money went directly toward another campaign commercial or a critical mailing. But with this allowance, it was different. We didn't have to do anything to earn it.

The message was simple: *You won. It's all paid for now.*

For the first time in my life I had an allowance—and it was a doozy—more than $1.2 million annually!

I definitely wasn't campaigning in Colorado anymore.

CLOSE ENCOUNTER AT THE CANNON

The parties began on the first evening with a Welcome Reception hosted by the Committee on House Administration. Everyone who was anyone in Congress was there. Guests of honor were Minority Leader Nancy Pelosi and Speaker John Boehner. All the faces I had seen on the cable news networks were now with me in the same room.

And what a room it was! The Cannon Caucus Room seemed designed to make everyone feel small, with fifty-foot-high ceilings and gorgeous tapestry-like drapes stretching from ceiling to floor. The official description gives some, but only some, sense of the airy grandeur the room evokes:

> Paired Corinthian pilasters give depth and interest to the high walls, and lead the eye to the elaborate ceiling. A molded plaster entablature, enriched with color and gilding, outlines the upper walls. The ceiling is decorated with a variety of classical motifs, including rosettes and a Greek key border.... The three-tiered chandeliers—original to the room and still in place—have unique glass shades surrounding the lights. Decorative motifs seen throughout the

Capitol Liberty caps, eagles, laurel wreaths, and fasces are sandblasted onto the globe shades...[1]

Waiters swarmed the rich, red carpets offering equally rich hors d'oeuvres. Fancy cheese and fruit trays decorated circular tables laden with salmon and tenderloin appetizers. Elegant orchids adorned the tables and wine flowed freely. The entire room swelled with the dulcet strains of a string quartet. Everything about the event said, *You are special.*

DON'T FORGET THE CONSTITUTION

The following night, the parties continued with Speaker John Boehner hosting another elegant soiree for Republicans in what is now known as Statuary Hall. The Hall was originally built for the House of Representatives and rebuilt after fire damaged the Capitol during the War of 1812. They used it until 1857 when the current chambers were completed.

The ornate room, one of the earliest examples of Greek revival architecture in America, had been built in the shape of an ancient amphitheater, complete with thirty-eight massive marble columns around the outside of the room. Today, statues of famous Americans stand at the edges of the black-and-white marbled floors, one in front of each column. They include such memorable figures as Ethan Allen, William Jennings Bryan, Henry Clay, Jefferson Davis, Barry Goldwater, Sequoyah, Daniel Webster, Brigham Young, and Sam Houston. During the day, natural sunlight enters through windows of the ornate rotunda high above the marbled floor. At night, a single elegant chandelier and recessed lighting give the space a hallowed feel that reminds all of its history.

I've been to a lot of fine restaurants in my day, but I had never seen a dinner setting as elegant as this one. Tables for eight featured dazzling floral centerpieces. Beef tenderloin once again topped the menu with all manner of fanciful foods and abundant wine. An Army choir of about eight singers wandered throughout the room, their voices harmonizing beautifully thanks to the unique acoustics of the fabled hall.

Other new members and I were seated with Republican Congresswoman Cathy McMorris Rodgers of Washington and her husband, a retired Navy commander. All of the new Republican members were in attendance, many with their spouses, along with about a dozen members of the Republican leadership.

As the event began, John Boehner stood and said a few words before introducing a historian from the Library of Congress to tell us more about the historic room. We were reminded again that we are elite: only 10,214 Americans have served in the U.S. House of Representatives since we gained our independence from Britain.

Several presidents had, in fact, been inaugurated in that very room. He pointed out plaques in the floor where former presidents once sat while serving in Congress—eight in all, including my favorite, Abraham Lincoln, and John Quincy Adams.

As the historian spoke, I was in awe at the history and splendor of it all, surrounded by gleaming marble, gilded ceilings, the finest food, and reminders of some of the greatest men and women our country has ever known. Then, he directed our attention upward.

He pointed to a larger-than-life statue of Lady Liberty. She stands looking down at what used to be the House chambers. To her right is the American eagle, a symbol of strength. To her left is a serpent coiled around part of a column, representing Sophia, the Greek goddess of wisdom. Lady Liberty extends her hand forward, reaching down toward us offering a scroll. That scroll, the historian noted, represents the Constitution of the United States of America. Lady Liberty offers it to the members of Congress as if to remind them, *Don't forget the Constitution when you vote.*

I renewed my intention to follow that very advice.

MY FIRST ACTION AS CLASS PRESIDENT

Shortly after arriving in Washington, the new members had elected me to serve as president of the Freshman Class, which made me their representative to the Republican leadership. The job of class president could be whatever I made of it—or nothing at all. As far as I was concerned, it was an opportunity to make a difference.

After my election, I was given a gavel and the responsibility of overseeing the election of freshmen to other offices, including positions on the House Steering Committee, which chooses committee assignments for all Republican members. Because the freshman class of 2010 was so large, they had been allowed three representatives on the Steering Committee. The 2012 class was smaller and only allowed one seat. For 2014, we were again slated to have only one representative on the Steering Committee, but I thought we should have more and asked for two committee seats.

During the glitzy party at Statuary Hall, I approached Speaker Boehner and made my case for having two new members on the Steering Committee. In his gruff smoker's voice, he answered curtly, "I'll think about it" and returned to his dinner. The next thing I knew, we had been granted the two seats. I felt like we were already getting something done.

TEAM AMERICA VS. TEAM REPUBLICAN

The following Monday, Candice Miller, chairman of the House Administration Committee, hosted a luncheon for us in the historic House dining room. Chris Christie, Republican governor of New Jersey, was the featured speaker. He delivered a clear message: that the fruits of victory were the ability to pass bills or bring money back to our districts that would help us win reelection. I confess, I had never been a big Christie fan, but I was astonished that his speech was not about winning for Team America, but rather winning for Team Republican by playing the Washington game.

I left that lunch frustrated, muttering to myself at the hypocrisy of it all. I ran for Congress as a Republican, and I share the values of the Republican Party far more than I do the values of the Democratic Party. But I was deeply offended to hear him say that we were all supposed to march in lockstep so we can get reelected, that our primary loyalty, in other words, was to do well for our party rather than to do well for America.

During the session, someone asked Christie about his presidential ambitions. He dodged that question but did ask us all to keep his remarks confidential. Not much chance of that. After the lunch, the freshmen stampeded to talk to the press waiting outside.

That very evening, I attended an after-hours event hosted by Republican Majority Leader Kevin McCarthy at the National Archives.

If you've seen the movie *National Treasure*, you've seen Hollywood's depiction of this building that houses our nation's most important documents. The actual rooms where the Declaration of Independence and Constitution are displayed are kept darker than what you see in the film. The low lighting makes for better document preservation and the ideal place for—you guessed it—another party.

This event had all the fineries I had come to expect after a week in Washington—fine food, fine wine, and fine décor—as well as special access to back rooms to view documents not on public display.

Once again, my clear impression was that we were meant to think that we were no longer like everyone else. As members of Congress, we were something special, and if we played the game the party leadership wanted us to play, our elite status could carry on indefinitely.

A SLICE OF DISRESPECT

By the time Orientation was finally over, I was eager to head home to Colorado. My wife and I checked out of the hotel and headed out for some real food—pizza. After all the steak, lobster, caviar, and smoked salmon, all we really wanted was a tasty slice of one of my favorite foods. Having lived on the East Coast as a child, I had developed a love for authentic Italian bakery pizza, and We the Pizza restaurant—just a few blocks from the Capitol—fit the bill.

When we arrived, two men in dark suits greeted us at the door and told us they had to wand us using hand-held metal detectors. I thought that was a little bizarre, even for Washington. We got our pizza and started up the stairs to the seating area only to find it blocked by another dark-suited, serious-looking fellow who said, "I'm sorry but you can't go upstairs." I saw his lapel pin and made the connection—Secret Service protective detail. Fortunately, it was a warm November day, so we grabbed some seats outside.

Just as we were about to dig in, two black SUVs pulled up, and more secret service agents emerged. Then a van pulled up, and snipers got out, grabbed their gear, and headed towards various buildings. Washington, D.C., police arrived, shut off the sidewalks and barricaded several lanes on Pennsylvania Avenue.

Security intercepted a truck trying to make a delivery at a nearby restaurant, and told the driver—no doubt given the scare of his life—to move along. My wife leaned over to me and asked in hushed tones, "Do you think this is for Biden?"

"No, this has to be for President Obama."

Two vans appeared and out popped a group of Hispanic teenagers who entered the restaurant. Two more black SUVs pulled up and President Obama stepped out of one of them. He walked past us, said, "Hey, guys," and headed into the pizzeria.

There were at least twenty DC Metro police and Secret Service agents on duty, not to mention the snipers and others we couldn't see. The pizza shop was serving as a photo op before President Obama announced his unconstitutional executive order granting amnesty to millions of illegal aliens.

Disgusted, I tweeted a picture I had taken of the president walking into the pizzeria with the message, "Lost my appetite." *The Denver Post* framed it as a personal attack on the president: "Ken Buck dishes out a slice of disrespect."[2]

The disrespect, it seemed to me, was from the president, who was spending tens of thousands of dollars for a photo op and then flouting our Constitution and loading the United States with yet another financial burden when we were already, at the time, $18 trillion in debt.

But few in Washington seemed to find it shocking at all.

CHAPTER 3

PLAY THE GAME— OR ELSE

"I'm going to make him an offer he can't refuse."

—Don Corleone, *The Godfather*

he killer bees—that's what one friend called us when he saw
us sitting together on the floor of the House of Representatives. Rod Blum (R-IA), Dave Brat (R-VA) and I have earned
a reputation for supporting free market solutions, less government
interference, and killing government waste. Dave Brat of Virginia and
I serve in what Washington insiders call "safe seats," districts that are
not targeted by the Democratic machine. Our colleague Rod Blum,
on the other hand, entered Congress in 2014 after a closely contested
election in Iowa's predominantly Democratic First Congressional
District.

Rod is a true conservative. He started the Congressional Term
Limits Caucus, introduced legislation to end lawmakers' access to
first class travel and luxury car leases, and introduced a bill to ban
members of Congress from ever becoming lobbyists. In his first

official action, Rod voted against then-House Speaker John Boehner on grounds that Boehner was failing to represent conservative ideals. Rod joined the Freedom Caucus and by most conservative scorecards Rod is easily one of the most principled conservatives in Congress. This, however, did not make him any friends among the Republican leadership.

The National Republican Congressional Committee announces a "Patriot" list each term, representing members who are in the toughest districts, are most at risk at the next election, and in need of the most fundraising help to maintain a Republican majority. When the list was published, Rod Blum's name was missing even though he had higher conservative ratings than any other congressman listed, several of whom had conservative ratings lower than that of liberal Democrat Maxine Waters of California.

To their credit, just before the 2016 election, Speaker Paul Ryan and Congressman Steve Stivers, deputy chairman of the NRCC, both attended fundraisers for Rod and helped him significantly. It might have been because they realized that the NRCC had made a mistake—or it might have been because, while Democrats were hoping to win back Rod's seat, Rod was already ahead in the polls and eventually won his race by eight points.

PRESSURE TO PLAY THE GAME

The pressure to play the game surfaces in subtle ways. Committees are where the real work of Congress gets done. If you want to serve on key committees, however, there are litmus tests.

I serve on the Judiciary Committee. What I discovered is that leadership looks for a certain *type* of representative to serve on the Judiciary Committee. For Republicans, he or she must be pro-life, pro-gun rights, and pro-immigration enforcement. On the other side of the aisle, Democrats insist on the opposite positions for their members on Judiciary. But not everybody wants to take strong ideological stands.

Members who want to play the D.C. game are often assigned to Appropriations, Energy and Commerce, or Ways and Means because they can raise more money for reelection as members of these influential committees, and they can avoid having tough ideological decisions on their voting record. Most important, to make it onto those committees—and stay there—members must be willing to play the game *and* do what leadership tells them to do.

During Orientation, I discovered firsthand how quickly, and how subtly, the screening process works. Incoming members are expected to let committee chairs know if they want to be on a committee. The Steering Committee is more likely to assign you to your desired committee if the chairman of that committee endorses you.

The three committees I was most interested in were Judiciary, Budget, and Oversight and Government Reform. I met with Republican Congressman Bob Goodlatte of Virginia, chairman of the Judiciary Committee, and my willingness to make tough votes seemed to work in my favor. When I met with Republican Congressman Tom Price of Georgia, chairman of the Budget Committee, my initial conversation was short and cordial. But when he followed up with me later, I got an education in party priorities.

He asked me if I would vote for the budget if I served on the committee.

I asked him the obvious question: "What if I don't like the budget?"

That was all he needed to know. He nodded and walked away. I learned later that Republican Congressmen Tim Huelskamp of Kansas and Justin Amash of Michigan had been booted from the Budget Committee before I arrived for not supporting a budget that raised the national debt even further.

THE PLAYGROUND BULLIES

One of our first votes in January of 2015 was electing the Speaker of the House. With our party in the majority we knew it was likely to be John Boehner, who had served as Speaker since January 2011, though three Republican congressmen decided to challenge him: Dan Webster and Ted Yoho of Florida and Louie Gohmert of Texas. It was a roll call vote and when our names were called we were to stand up and announce our choice for Speaker of the House. When I was called, I stood and said, "John Boehner." (My constituents hated that vote of mine more than any other that I've taken. The longer I was there, the better I understood why.)

The outcome was never really in doubt. Boehner won easily with 216 votes. His opponents combined for only seventeen votes. What happened next revealed the appalling level of pettiness of the Republican leadership. It wasn't enough for Boehner to win; dissenters had to be punished.

The leadership booted Congressman Webster, the most popular of the non-Boehner candidates, from the influential Rules Committee. (The Florida Senate, controlled by Republicans, then redrew his congressional district boundaries, forcing him to run for reelection in a less favorable district.[1]) As president of the freshman class, one of my duties was to schedule new congressmen to preside over the assembly in the House chair. I was told by Boehner's staff not to schedule anyone who had voted against him as speaker. Even pettier than that, some members who voted against Boehner had their dining room privileges revoked. When Congressman Brat tried to make reservations for a group of constituents at the House dining room, he was told that he could not make reservations and that the dining room was full. He took his constituents to the dining room anyway, found it almost empty, and muscled his way in.

The Republican leadership seemed far more interested in imposing its will over Republican congressmen than it did in tackling the national debt and other pressing concerns. The examples are legion. For instance, members of Congress routinely go on official trips called CODELs (Congressional Delegations) that are authorized by committee chairs. But in the hands of leadership such authorization is just another weapon. When Republican Congresswoman Cynthia Lummis of Wyoming voted against Republican Hal Rogers of Kentucky for the Appropriations chair, her scheduled trip to South Sudan was abruptly cancelled in retaliation. Similarly, Republican Steve King of Iowa had an approved, scheduled trip to meet Egyptian President Abdel Fattah el-Sisi to discuss the persecution of Christians in Egypt. But Speaker Boehner rescinded the approval, because King hadn't voted for him. King kept his commitment to meet with the Egyptian president, paying for the trip himself.

"My vote card doesn't belong to John Boehner," said King.

A Republican aide rationalized the Speaker's action this way: "Taxpayer-funded travel and other perks go to those members who *deserve to be rewarded*, not members who *oppose the broader GOP team...*" (emphasis mine).[2] In other words, taxpayer funds only go to those who play the game.

King has publicly acknowledged he is not the only one to be the target of such retaliation: "Some people capitulate, some people rebel. Others try to hold principled statesmanlike ground." But it can be quite expensive.

The same thing happened to Republican Mark Meadows of North Carolina when he opposed Boehner and the leadership in 2015. Meadows had been approved to lead a trip to the Democratic Republic of the Congo. After Boehner was reelected, Meadows was told not only would he not lead the trip, but he couldn't even go. According to Meadows, Republican Majority Leader Kevin McCarthy confirmed this to a shocked Congresswoman Karen Bass (D-CA), who couldn't believe it and had gone to ask McCarthy about it herself. Sure enough, Meadows was grounded for not playing the game.[3]

Let me be clear: both parties are guilty of this level of petty punishment and manipulation. But while you might cynically expect that from the Democrats, who are the party of big government, it was disappointing, to say the least, that so many Republicans—supposedly coming from the party of fiscal restraint, smaller government, and less regulation—seemed far more interested in gaining political favors than following principled policies.

CARDINAL CASTIGATION

One of my striking lessons in the bizarre dysfunction of Congress took place in my first year as a congressman when I offered an amendment to an appropriations bill. I wanted to give the Bureau of Alcohol, Tobacco, and Firearms (ATF) the authority to restore, at its discretion, the Second Amendment rights of reformed felons.

At first glance, of course, it's easy to see why we might not want felons to own guns. But in reality, there could be any number of reasons why an exception should be made. For example, one constituent explained to me that he had written a bad check at the age of eighteen and accepted a felony plea deal in order to get probation and avoid jail time. However, because it was a felony violation, he had been stripped of his Second Amendment right to "keep and bear arms." After forty years of working hard, raising a family, and living an honest life, he wanted to go hunting with his grandson, but couldn't legally possess a firearm.

It only made sense to me that the ATF should be able to review such situations and reinstate those rights as they saw fit. Unfortunately, long before I arrived in Congress, Democratic Senator Chuck Schumer had repeatedly offered an amendment—so often that it was now automatically inserted in every year's Appropriations bill—that would block such proposals by denying the ATF necessary funding. I wanted to offer an amendment to strike that language and restore the citizen's right to make an appeal.

Apparently, my simple amendment created quite a stir, even though it didn't reach the floor of the House until late one night around 11:00 pm. I was joined by a "cardinal."

A cardinal is a subcommittee chairman on the Appropriations Committee, but some of them seem to think they're divinely inspired and assigned power from on high. He spent no less than forty-five minutes haranguing me from the House floor.

"You are going to singlehandedly cause us to lose the majority," he said repeatedly. "You're not playing on this team, Buck. You are a disgrace! You're a Republican! If we're in the minority, it's going to be *your* fault! You're never going to get reelected if you keep this up!"

"You *are* going to withdraw this amendment!" the cardinal finally insisted.

"I am not going to withdraw the amendment, sir."

"You are going to withdraw this amendment! This is a disgrace!"

The House was nearly deserted at that late hour, but it eventually dawned on me that neither the Democrats nor the Republicans present wanted to face what they considered a controversial vote that would be captured on C-SPAN.

When my turn came, I stood and offered my amendment. The member in the Speaker's chair said, "All in favor say *aye.*" I said aye. "All opposed say *no.*" And the room was silent. The acting Speaker at the time shot a puzzled look at the cardinal. He shrugged back and the speaker said, "The *ayes* have it."

"Congratulations!" the cardinal said to me after the vote. *What are you talking about? You harassed me in front of everyone and now you congratulate me?*

Both parties thought I was trying to rock the boat, but all I wanted was to restore funding for a common sense appeals process.

Unfortunately, it is quite common for cardinals to bully members. Cynthia Lummis (R-WY) experienced a similar verbal beating when she simply tried to do her job.

Separate from an appropriations bill is a narrative that details exactly how the money will be spent. Although she had been briefed on the contents of the bill prior to the Interior, Environment, and Related Agencies subcommittee meeting, she had not been permitted to see the report language. When she walked into the committee room, both the report language and the bill were waiting. The subcommittee cardinal told her to vote for the bill, and she did. Then she was told she could not take the report language with her. In other words, the subcommittee cardinal required her to vote for the bill *before* reading it—and then wouldn't let her read it *after* the vote either.

Nevertheless, Lummis picked up her copy of the report language and walked out with it. Staffers from the committee soon tracked her down and harassed her, insisting she give it back. She adamantly refused.

The committee cardinal not only berated her from the House floor, he swore at her, thundering, "God damn it! You take that back!"

Lummis replied, "I want to *read* what I voted for!"[4] It only got uglier from there. The cardinal was among Speaker Boehner's inner circle, and leadership pressure forced Lummis to resign from the Appropriations Committee.

PAY-TO-PLAY

Representatives want committee seats for a variety of reasons, some of them honorable, some of them not. For some members, committee assignments aren't so much about public service as they are about raising one's public profile—and attracting special interest donations to one's campaign fund. Because congressional leadership understands that self-interest motivates many members to serve on committees, they leverage that desire by unofficially ranking the committees.

Numerous high-level members of the Republican House leadership have confirmed to me that committees are ranked. The ranking system is understood by members, though seldom spoken of. Committees are assigned letters—A, B, or C—based on how important they are deemed to be by leadership.

There are five A committees in the House: Appropriations, Ways and Means, Energy and Commerce, Rules, and Financial Services. Both parties use committee appointments to raise money. If you want to serve on a committee in Congress, you have to pay for the privilege.

Here's how it works for Republicans. If you want to serve on a committee, you have to raise money for the National Republican Congressional Committee (NRCC). The amount varies depending on the committee and role. For example, to serve on a B or C level committee, a GOP House freshman member must raise $220,000 every two years. I paid that amount to the NRCC in my first term in Congress, but now must pay more than double that amount. Veteran members on A committees must raise more than twice that amount—$450,000. That's right, almost half a million dollars to do what the people elected them to do.

Republican representatives from districts deemed to be at risk by the NRCC get their dues discounted by at least 30 percent. Twelve Republican members were designated in 2015 to be part of this "Patriot" program,[5] but other members whose districts were equally at risk, like Rod Blum, were not included in the program, because they did not play the leadership's game.

As it is, some members of Congress spend at least half their time fundraising to keep their dues paid and campaign coffers full. If you become the chair of a B committee—congratulations—you're now expected to raise $875,000 a year for the NRCC. Chairing an A committee means you must raise $1.2 million. The higher your role in the House leadership, the higher the price tag:

Deputy Whip	$2.5 million
Conference Chair	$5 million
Whip	$5 million
Majority Leader	$10 million
Speaker	$20 million

When representatives don't pay their "dues" or fall behind, they are pressured to pay up—or else. It's happened to me, and I've heard similar stories from countless others.

Candidates' ability to raise cash is largely influenced by how well they play the game with leadership, and if you don't pay your dues, you can't use the NRCC call suites (or other benefits like the NRCC recording studios) to raise money.

To make matters worse, the NRCC got caught using those pay-to-play funds to support a recount effort against a conservative candidate in a Republican primary in 2016. When Andy Biggs ran to replace the retiring Matt Salmon in Arizona's Fifth District, he narrowly defeated the moderate opponent in the primary, former GoDaddy executive Christine Jones.

The NRCC has a longstanding policy to not meddle in primary elections, a promise affirmed to me in person by leadership. Yet the NRCC paid more than $300,000 in legal fees to fund Jones's recount effort. After Biggs won the recount by twenty-seven votes and won again in the general election, the NRCC offered to lower his dues and write a check to his campaign for the same amount that they gave his opponent.

I felt the same sting from my own party in 2010 when the National Republican Senatorial Committee (NRSC) gave my opponent $500,000 in the primary race. She used that money to label me as anti-woman, a theme my Democratic opponent was only too happy to capitalize on in the general election.

Committee assignments, then, are less about qualifications than they are about cash—or, to put it another way, cash is the chief qualification you need. Aside from his outstanding policy credentials,

House Speaker Paul Ryan is certainly well qualified for his position—
he raised more than $50 million in 2016.

Serving on certain committees can also mean a lot of donations
for representatives. A recent review of fundraising patterns over the
last two decades revealed that members of *some* House committees
rake in more donor cash than others. The study concluded that getting
"on Ways and Means boosts your PAC fundraising levels by
$208,315" and "your out-of-state itemized fundraising totals by
$233,742...." While joining "Financial Services produces a boost of
$101,695 to PAC contributions and a boost of $140,334 to your out-
of-state contributions.... Joining Energy and Commerce yields a
statistically significant boost of $72,933 to your PAC contributions."[6]

It's easy to see why the three committees mentioned above are all
considered to be A committees. Corporate fortunes can be made or
lost by legislation that affects their industries. Consequently, generous
campaign donations often flow to members of these committees. For
example, the financial, real estate, and insurance industries contributed more than $29 million to members of the Financial Services
Committee, more than $16 million to members of the Ways and
Means, and more than $8 million to members of Energy and Com-
merce, either through Political Action Committees (PACs) or to individuals.[7] That's one reason why these congressional committee
assignments are so valuable to so many in the House.

Corporations use this leverage to get what they want included in
legislation. For example, one biotechnology firm seemed to work the
broken system well during the "fiscal cliff crisis" of 2013 according
to the *New York Times*:

> Just two weeks after pleading guilty in a major federal
> fraud case, Amgen, the world's largest biotechnology firm,

scored a largely unnoticed coup on Capitol Hill: Lawmakers inserted a paragraph into the "fiscal cliff" bill that did not mention the company by name but strongly favored one of its drugs.

The language buried in Section 632 of the law delays a set of Medicare price restraints on a class of drugs that includes Sensipar, a lucrative Amgen pill used by kidney dialysis patients.

The provision gives Amgen an additional two years to sell Sensipar without government controls. The news was so welcome that the company's chief executive quickly relayed it to investment analysts. But it is projected to cost Medicare up to $500 million over that period.

Amgen, which has a small army of 74 lobbyists in the capital, was the only company to argue aggressively for the delay, according to several congressional aides of both parties.[8]

I am not opposed to lobbyists. Everyone, both individuals and groups, has a right to petition Congress. But when the request is closely tied to donations and results in last-minute legislative perks, the people's trust in government deteriorates. And because the fiscal cliff bill was forced upon Congress at the final hour, written in secret behind closed doors, most members didn't find out about this change until it was too late, if they ever knew about it at all.

House leadership doles out these influential committee assignments to those who play the game. After Speaker Boehner announced his retirement in 2015, Ways and Means Committee Chairman Paul Ryan met with the Freedom Caucus to earn our support for his effort to become Speaker. Paul met with about thirty of us in the Ways and

Means Committee conference room, right off the House floor, while the press waited outside.

We had a good conversation. When we told Paul that leadership was discriminating against conservatives, he asked us, "How many of you are on Ways and Means?" He was surprised that *none* of us were; clearly, he was not in the loop about Boehner's war on conservatives.

The real partisanship in Washington isn't between political parties or about political principle; it is *within* parties, where leaders punish members who don't play the game. In Congress, the consensus has been, it's better to sink the nation with debt than rock the boat with reform. If we're going to drain the swamp, we need to change that.

CHAPTER 4

CRISIS OF CHARACTER

"Public virtue cannot exist in a Nation without private Virtue, and public Virtue is the only Foundation of Republics."

—John Adams[1]

Before my election, Congress had passed a continuing resolution (CR) to keep the government operating from October through December 2014. In mid-November, after the elections, President Obama issued an unconstitutional executive order that essentially offered a form of amnesty to millions of illegal immigrants.

When the House returned for its lame-duck session, before the arrival of the new Congress in January, leadership offered a 1,600-page omnibus spending bill that had to be passed quickly to avoid a government shutdown. To gain conservative votes, Speaker Boehner threatened not to fund the department that would be executing the president's executive order, the Department of Homeland Security. A separate continuing resolution would fund Homeland Security only until March of 2015.

To win over Republican votes for the Cromnibus, as the hybrid legislation came to be called, Boehner promised to fight Obama's immigration order "tooth and nail." His promise proved to be a symbolic gesture to get the votes he needed in December and nothing more. When he changed his position on the CR in early 2015, it was a blatant violation of his promise to stand and fight against Obama's unconstitutional executive power grab.

Boehner first requested a three-week extension in late February 2015. A federal judge in Texas had already blocked the executive order from being implemented, so I voted to give Boehner the benefit of the doubt. I knew no harm could come of the extra time. Nevertheless, he could only get a seven-day extension passed with so much of his party in open revolt. A week later, Boehner completely caved to Democratic demands and worked with them to pass DHS funding. I voted against the DHS funding because it included money to implement Obama's unconstitutional immigration action.

Nearly two-thirds of Republicans joined me in rejecting Boehner's surrender. The House Republicans had a long-standing but informal rule that before permitting a floor vote, the Speaker had to ensure that the majority of his party supported a bill, which we plainly didn't.

Making common cause with the Democrats rather than his own party, Boehner retaliated against Republicans who had voted against him with attack ads that accused Congressmen Jim Jordan of Ohio, Tim Huelskamp of Kansas, and Jim Bridenstine of Oklahoma of putting America's "security at risk." The ads were run by the American Action Network (AAN), led by Mike Shields, former Republican National Committee chief of staff. AAN shared office space, and even a spokesman, with the Congressional Leadership Fund, a Boehner "super PAC."[2]

When Tim Huelskamp tried to confront Boehner about the ads on the House floor, the Speaker avoided him. According to Huelskamp, "He just walked by; he didn't have a comment.... I was waiting to ask him about it. In Kansas, we wouldn't do that. In my family, if you've got a problem with someone, you have the wherewithal to take it up with them."[3]

By March 2015, I had witnessed Speaker Boehner commit three character-compromising acts. He went back on his word to fight the president's unconstitutional executive order "tooth and nail." By doing so, he confirmed his critics' worst suspicions that he had made the promise only to get votes for the continuing resolution omnibus spending bill, not because he opposed the president's actions or wanted to uphold the Constitution and defend the integrity of Congress. He also violated a revered rule of the House to the detriment of his own party, and to the detriment of conservative principles, without explaining his reasoning. And, finally, he unleashed friendly fire on the allies he needed in the future. He failed to recognize that not everyone in the House shared his desire to maintain power at the expense of the American people.

AS A WHALE THROUGH A NET

I knew Congress and corruption were two words long associated with each other, but it was still shocking to see it firsthand. I was old enough to remember the Abscam case in the 1980s when the FBI ran an undercover sting, posing as Arab Sheiks trying to bribe congressmen. Seven members went to federal prison. I remembered the Congressional Post Office Scandal of the early 1990s that sent Dan Rostenkowski, chairman of the House Ways and Means Committee, to federal prison for conspiracy to embezzle House Post Office money through stamps and postal vouchers. I remembered the 1992 House banking investigation that found 450 members (past and current) were overdrawn on their checking accounts. Six members were convicted on related charges and twenty-two others were punished by the House Ethics Committee.

While the scandals pouring out of Washington seemed continuous, I assumed it was just a few bad apples. Once I arrived in Congress, I realized that while there are *some* good apples, there are a *lot* of rotten ones—and the whole apple barrel itself is rotten. Within my first two years, four members were indicted. Republican Congressman Michael Grimm of New York pleaded guilty to tax evasion. Democratic Congressman Chaka Fattah of Pennsylvania was convicted on twenty-three counts of racketeering, fraud, and corruption. Democratic Congresswoman Corrine Brown was charged with fraud.[4] And two days after the 2016 election, federal charges were filed against Republican Congressman Aaron Schock of Illinois who had already resigned after allegations of financial misdealings.[5]

In only the few years prior to my arrival, Republican Congressman Trey Radel of Florida had been convicted of cocaine possession.[6] Democratic Congresswoman Laura Richardson of California had been found guilty of destroying evidence and tampering with witness testimony and five other charges by the House Ethics Committee.[7] Democratic Congressman Jesse Jackson Jr. of Illinois had pled guilty to wire and mail fraud involving $750,000 of campaign money.[8] Arizona Republican Rick Renzi had been convicted on seventeen counts, including fraud, conspiracy, extortion, racketeering, and money laundering.[9] Republican Mark Souder of Indiana resigned to dodge an investigation into an extramarital affair with a female staffer.[10] New York Republican Chris Lee sent pictures of his torso to a woman via Craigslist using his official congressional email.[11]

Louisiana Republican Vance McAllister was caught on camera kissing a married staffer.[12] And who can forget the FBI seizing $90,000 from the freezer of Louisiana Democrat William J. Jefferson, or Democratic Congressman Anthony Weiner's "sexting" habits, or former Republican Dennis Hastert paying hush money to hide his own sexual misconduct?

Our second president, John Adams, reminded us that self-government is dependent on personal morality. "We have no government," he wrote, "armed with power capable of contending with human passions unbridled by morality and religion. Avarice, ambition, revenge, or gallantry would break the strongest cords of our constitution as a whale goes through a net. Our Constitution was made only for a moral and religious people. It is wholly inadequate to the government of any other."[13]

We were lucky that our founders understood this, and for the most part were such men. George Washington perhaps above all provided the model for the self-sacrificing, dutiful, moral hero. We've come a long way since then, and unfortunately in recent decades we've been going in the wrong direction. Political questions are, in the end, moral questions, and unless this country sends to Congress moral men we will not have moral laws and moral leadership.

THE COWARD'S WAY OUT

Morality isn't just about legality; it's about doing what's right. Corruption, for a congressman, doesn't have to involve illegality; it can be as simple as, and unfortunately as common as, promoting your own interests (chiefly reelection) over the interests of the country (fiscal responsibility). I've asked numerous members why they voted for bloated omnibus bills that plunge us further into debt. What I get in reply is an agreement that the bill was bad for America—but also that it was good for them *personally*. And that generally means not that they received illegal payoffs but that they delivered pork-barrel projects to their states that would be popular with the press and with their constituents. Or it could mean that they brought home the bacon for special interest lobbyists who are powerful in their state or nationally. Special interests represented in the 2015 omnibus bill ranged from bakers to green energy proponents to Puerto Rican rum distillers and just about everything in between.

It's easier for members to rationalize voting for an irresponsible omnibus bill when they can point to a special favor for a constituent, a special interest group, or their district. But the truth is they are just excuses to stay in Congress longer. Will Rogers was right when he joked, "These fellows in Washington wouldn't be so serious and particular if they only had to vote on what they thought was good for the majority of the people in the U.S. That would be a cinch. But what makes it hard for them is every time a bill comes up they have things to decide that have nothing to do with the merit of the bill. The principal thing is of course: What will this do for me personally back home?"[14]

Today, no one wants to say we can't keep putting deficit spending on the national credit card, because congressmen think they're more likely to get reelected through pork than fiscal prudence and the moral principle of not burdening the next generation with unbearable debt. That's the coward's way out. But Congress currently rewards cowards. A simple fix—a requirement that the federal government have a balanced budget—would do a lot to fix this. It would force members of Congress to make the hard decisions they're elected to make; and it would encourage members of Congress to tell the truth to their constituents, that if they want, for instance, more defense spending, they

have to be willing to accept cuts in welfare spending. Or if they want
to leave Social Security unreformed, then we need to raise taxes.

Right now, too many people in Congress would rather let Social
Security collapse at some point in the future than risk being thrown
out of office for solving that problem now. They would rather accept
sequestration cuts (which are automatic and remove them from
responsibility) than make hard decisions about what our spending
priorities should be. They would rather pretend that we can balance
the budget with taxes only on the "rich" than confront the reality that
we can't tax our way out of a $20 trillion debt. If Congress were
required to balance the federal budget, however, members could
campaign on the reality that cuts and compromise are required of all.

GOVERNMENT BY CRISIS

When he was president-elect, Obama's chief of staff, Rahm Eman-
uel, said, "You never let a serious crisis go to waste." That idea isn't
new. Frightening the people in order to enlarge the role of government,
or coordinating a crisis to get your way with a legislature is a common
political tactic.

When Nancy Pelosi was Speaker of the House, she would delay
appropriations bills until the end of the fiscal year, forcing members
to vote on a single piece of omnibus legislation (rather than twelve
properly prepared and vetted appropriations bills).

Only the Speaker's closest allies knew what was in the bill, yet
members either had to approve it immediately or face the fallout of a
government shutdown.

Consequently, we ended up with a series of continuing resolutions,
legislative Band-Aids applied to keep government alive from crisis to
crisis. On some occasions she would keep the House in session right up

to Christmas Eve when members wanted to be home with their families. It was all an attempt to bully the representatives of the people to do the will of the Democratic congressional cartel. And it worked.

Republicans rightly criticized Pelosi for her tactics, and yet when the Republicans regained the majority in 2010, John Boehner did exactly the same thing. After promising to restore regular order, he used the same crisis manipulation tactics to bully members to comply. He continued to draft spending bills in the Speaker's office and dump them on the House floor at the last minute. He continued to negotiate independently with Senate leadership and President Obama, thereby bypassing the House of Representatives, the voice of the people.

For example, he negotiated an increase to the debt ceiling in July 2011 that effectively raised our national debt by $2 trillion. The deal also formed a Joint Select Committee to suggest ways to cut spending or face automatic budget cuts. The committee consisted of six Democrats and six Republicans, three from each legislative chamber, for a total of twelve.

Not surprisingly, they failed to agree, and House members were forced to return to Washington over the Christmas holiday and pass legislation that Boehner had single-handedly negotiated with the Obama administration. Not long before midnight on December 31, most House members went along with the scheme.

These are the games played by those who want to avoid making tough choices. These are the tactics used by men and women of low character—in both parties—to pressure members of Congress to comply.

THE REPUBLICAN LEGACY

What bothers me most about the moral corruption in Congress is how it betrays the Republican Party's history and heritage. Until fairly recently, the Republican Party stood boldly for freedom. It was born as an anti-slavery party, led by Abraham Lincoln. Under Theodore Roosevelt it was an anti-socialist and anti-crony capitalist party. Under Dwight Eisenhower and Richard Nixon it promoted civil rights (just as it had done in the 1860s and 1870s, after the Civil War).

Republican President Ronald Reagan stood not only in defense of freedom at home but stood in Berlin and dared Mr. Gorbachev to "tear down this wall" and bring freedom to millions of people across the globe.

The great Republican Party leaders of the past did not shy away from controversy or hard decisions. But in recent years, the Republican Party has rushed to become little more than a watered-down version of the Democratic Party—only worse in terms of hypocrisy: talking the conservative talk in order to get elected, but then walking the Democratic walk of big government in order to cavort and wallow in the Washington swamp.

I guess that makes sense if your sole rationale for being a congressman is to enjoy the perks of power. But what has it gotten the rest of us, the American people? The answer is massive, unsustainable debt and a litany of related problems that no one has shown much interest in solving.

Our crushing debt isn't merely a fiscal challenge or an economic problem. It is a potential moral catastrophe that will ruin the prospects of our children and grandchildren. Unless we address this enormous problem now—as Republicans addressed other great problems in the past—we won't be arguing about a crisis in the future, because our nation won't have a future at all.

CHAPTER 5

BEATING THE BELTWAY BULLIES

"There is no distinctly American criminal class—except Congress."

—Mark Twain

I n January 2015, a group of Republican congressional conservatives—I was among them—set up the Freedom Caucus. Unlike the Republican Study Committee, which had started as a conservative caucus but was open to all and therefore had been subverted by the Republican leadership (which had encouraged moderates to join), the Freedom Caucus was to be a closed, invitation-only caucus. Republican leadership needed 218 votes to get anything done, half of the House plus one. The aim of our new Freedom Caucus was to get leverage for common sense solutions and conservative principles. We soon had about thirty-seven members, which was enough to deny Boehner a majority if everyone voted together. This gave conservatives leverage because Democrats almost always vote as a bloc against anything Republicans want.

The first big test of the Freedom Caucus arrived when Speaker Boehner tried to force us to agree to give President Obama more power (or what had been known as "trade promotion authority") to negotiate trade deals with foreign countries. We didn't think that was a good idea.

TRADING EVILS

Now trade promotion authority itself is not a bad thing. Beginning in 1974, Congress had granted special authority to the president to facilitate trade deals in the best interest of America and agreed to expedite the approval of those deals. The idea was to give trading partners reassurance that Congress, and special interests represented in Congress, would not amend trade agreements negotiated by the executive branch. Congress can give guidelines to the president on the front end, but only a *yes* or *no* vote on the final agreement—thumbs-up or thumbs-down.

This fast-track authority (as it has been called) was allowed to expire in 2007 when Democrats controlled both the House and the Senate and George W. Bush was the Republican president. Subsequently, the Obama administration began negotiating a Trans-Pacific Partnership agreement assuming that the executive's trade promotion authority would be reinstated eventually.[1] In April 2015, several senators introduced a bill to reinstate and expand that authority. The Bipartisan Congressional Trade Priorities and Accountability Act of 2015 cleared the Senate in May and arrived in the House to mixed reviews.

I had many concerns, frankly, about granting the president more authority to negotiate anything. President Obama had just negotiated with the world's largest sponsor of terrorism—Iran. He had agreed to give $150 billion to the country responsible for the improvised explosive devices maiming and killing thousands of American soldiers in Iraq. His secret nuclear agreement with Iran had side deals he failed to reveal to Congress; and the agreement itself—though a treaty in all but name—was not deemed a treaty so that Obama could avoid objections from Congress and the Constitutional stipulation that treaties be ratified by the Senate. Then-Secretary of State John Kerry actually told Congress that the deal was not a treaty because "you can't pass a treaty anymore,"[2] or at least not one as bad as the Obama administration negotiated.

I was not alone in my concern. Many of us did not believe President Obama had proven himself to be trustworthy. As this trade promotion authority bill came before the House, we balked at giving President Obama or any future president broader powers to make even worse deals. At least thirty-three other Republicans agreed with me.

What came next was a procedural issue. We vote on rules that allow a bill to come to the floor of the House. The majority party controls the process, if all members vote on party lines. Of course, as freshmen, we had all been told that we should never vote against our party on procedural motions.

In this instance, however, the rule was a *self-executing rule*, which meant that by voting for the rule, we were actually voting for legislation that would be automatically enacted if the rule passed. Boehner and the Republican leadership had set it up this way to, once again, help representatives on both sides of the aisle avoid tough votes.

Obama had insisted that he would only accept a Trade Promotion Authority (TPA) bill that included an increase in funding of the Trade Adjustment Assistance (TAA) program, which is usually described as a training program for American workers adversely affected by trade agreements. Really it is a payoff to labor unions. Many Republicans considered the TAA to be nothing more than another opportunity to spend more money.

This particular rule split the legislation that had passed the Senate into three smaller bills:

1) A TAA bill *with* Medicare spending cuts,

2) A TAA bill *without* any Medicare cuts, and

3) The TPA legislation itself

Emma Dumain at *Roll Call* summed up the purpose of the complex rule:

The rule would state that, once passed, the Medicare offset provision also *would be considered passed*, canceling out the need to hold an actual vote on the Medicare language. By voting against the rule, Democrats also could vote against the Medicare language, then vote on TAA without the Medicare language.[3] [emphasis mine]

In other words, once the rule was passed, the first vote—to fund TAA with Medicare spending cuts "would be considered passed" *without members actually voting on it.* In this way, *no one had to go on record* as cutting funding for the elderly—even though the reality was that nothing would actually be cut because Congress has ways of shifting money around to cover itself from criticism.

This wasn't simply a procedural motion. Legislative action was inserted into the rule—and we were required to vote for a rule that would increase spending *and* expand an out-of-control president's authority.

I discussed this vote with Republican Congressman Mark Meadows of North Carolina and we both refused to go along with the madness. The whole purpose of this vote was to play the bipartisan game of increasing spending and federal power while giving members plausible deniability by disguising what we were actually voting on.[4]

Thirty-four Republicans, mostly Freedom Caucus members, said *no*. If we stuck together we had enough votes to bring the Republican total under the 218-vote majority needed to pass the rule.

THE VOTE

As the time came to cast our votes, the party whips, members whose job it is to turn out votes, scurried to get the majority they needed. Speaker Boehner realized the vote could be close, and the usual bullying tactics weren't working, at least not yet.

Pete Sessions, chairman of the powerful Rules Committee, and someone I considered a friend, tried to talk me out of opposing the party leadership.

Pete's father William had become director of the FBI the same year I started as a prosecutor, in 1987. A former federal judge and federal prosecutor himself, Director Sessions developed a reputation for being non-partisan in the pursuit of justice, opening the hiring process at the Bureau to more women and minorities, and always putting his country first. Sessions didn't compromise with the D.C. power structure. He paid the price for it. Under Sessions the Bureau operated as an independent investigating agency with the highest integrity, a stark contrast to the days of J. Edgar Hoover. He had an acrimonious relationship with the attorneys general he worked with and authorized cases regardless of the political consequences. Forty-eight hours after Director Sessions opened an investigation of high-ranking Justice Department officials, he suddenly became the subject of an ethics investigation. President Bill Clinton ultimately fired Director Sessions over minor allegations, which paled in comparison to Clinton's own activities.

When I arrived in Congress I struck up a friendship with Pete Sessions. I had respected his dad's willingness to put principle over party. Pete was one of the architects of the Republican majority in 2010 and often referred to me as his little brother. While Pete voted with Boehner to keep his chairmanship on Rules, he treated conservatives fairly and found ways to achieve harmony within the Republican conference.

When Pete came up to me and asked me to vote for the TPA rule, I paused out of respect for him. Finally, I looked at him and said I just couldn't do it. He told me I should always vote my conscience. I appreciated knowing there were still some good people in Congress.

The next person who tried to whip my vote wasn't nearly as pleasant.

Boehner himself came striding up the center aisle towards me, grimacing and clearly unhappy with how the vote was going.

"Buck! Put your card in and vote yes!"

"Sorry, sir, I'm going to vote against this one."

"*What?*"

"I'm going to vote against this one," I repeated, and reached for my voting card.

Boehner stormed off, looking for someone else's vote to change.

As the votes were being cast, it looked pretty certain that we had enough Republicans to block Boehner. But Boehner and Republican leadership did something unprecedented: they started whipping *Democrats* to vote for the bill, because they knew that many Democrats wanted to pass the TPA and TAA, but needed political cover.

The rule passed by a vote of 217 to 212. It was a "bipartisan victory" to spend billions of dollars while dodging responsibility for that decision.

THE FALLOUT

We all knew there would be consequences for our decision to stand on principle, but the level of vindictive retaliation still surprised me. Three members of the Republican Whip team were removed from their positions—Trent Franks of Arizona, Cynthia Lummis of Wyoming, and Steve Pearce of New Mexico.

Cynthia Lummis knew what was coming and left the whip team voluntarily. Boehner, she told me, "clearly couldn't give a rip about Wyoming and its member of Congress," and had no sympathy for a conservative whip that thought members should vote their conscience. But her resignation wasn't good enough for Boehner. The leadership announced that she had been fired, along with Trent Franks and Steve Pearce.

At the next meeting of all House Republicans, Speaker Boehner called members out publicly in front of their peers to berate and humiliate them. Our committee chairs met with us individually, telling us we would lose our committee assignments if we voted against another rule, and that the NRCC—the recipient of millions in members' committee dues—would never help us again.

Candidly, that second threat was worthless to members of the Freedom Caucus because the NRCC didn't help any of us anyway. You have to be almost 100 percent loyal to Republican leadership and in a competitive seat to receive any financial help from the NRCC. Freedom Caucus members contributed a lot of money to the NRCC, but we received no financial help in return. So losing NRCC support was a symbolic punishment, but losing committee assignments was a real threat. Congressman Tim Huelskamp of Kansas, for one, was defeated in his 2016 primary in no small part because Boehner ousted him from his seat on the House Agricultural Committee and supported his primary opponent.

Within days of his vote against the rule, Congressman Mark Meadows of North Carolina got a visit from House Oversight and Government Reform Committee Chairman Jason Chaffetz of Utah. Meadows served as Government Operations subcommittee chairman. Chaffetz had two issues with Meadows: voting against the rule and not paying his dues to the NRCC.

Chaffetz told Meadows he had to be a team player. He told him he had to give money "across the street," meaning to the NRCC. The fact was that Meadows had a $21,000 check ready to give but had paused when leadership began to run attack ads against his fellow Republicans. He wanted assurances that his own party wouldn't run attack ads against him—hardly an unreasonable request. When Chaffetz told him the Speaker didn't have any control over the ads, Meadows told him that was nonsense. It was very clear where the message was coming from.

Chaffetz told Meadows he couldn't have him voting against the rule and not giving to the NRCC. So he took Mark's chairmanship away. Meadows had been an exemplary chairman to that point, fully engaged with one of the best attendance records on the committee. He told me he struggled to see how the two issues were connected with his performance as chair of the subcommittee. Chaffetz told Meadows that Majority Leader Kevin McCarthy (R-CA) had made it very clear to him that such behavior could not be tolerated, and he was sure that Boehner would support the decision. For voting his conscience and the way his constituents wanted him to vote, Meadows was stripped of his chairmanship.

But this time, the blowback from angry members of Congress and outraged citizens forced leadership to walk that back, and Chaffetz reinstated Meadows.[5]

SURPRISE ATTACK

Nevada Congressman Crescent Hardy, a fellow freshman, asked if he could talk with me. We walked together from the Capitol to the Cannon Building where we both had offices on the fourth floor.

"Ken," he spoke somewhat hesitantly as we approached my office, "there's been a group of us who've met and—we're going to ask for your resignation as Class President. We just don't think you're doing a good job."

I tried not to laugh. After all, there was no job description for class president in the House. The position was what anyone chose to make of it. I had been waiting to see what form the consequences of my vote would take, and now I knew. This was about payback for voting against the rule, pure and simple.

"Ok, you asked," I said with a shrug, "and I'm not going to resign."

"Well, in that case, we're going to have a special meeting to recall you," he replied, then paused before adding, "and I'm thinking of running for the position." Once again I smiled as more of the plan came to light.

"Ok, if you've got the votes," I responded with a quick nod, "then I guess you can do it." He kept talking, seemingly gaining confidence with each revelation.

"We've gone to the House parliamentarian and asked him what the procedure is to recall an officer in the class," Hardy said, "and we've got the procedure down."

"Ok." There wasn't much more to say. We parted ways.

An email went out to all the Republican freshman members—except to me and the freshmen most supportive of me—to inform them of an important meeting to discuss the performance of the class president. The meeting was scheduled by Congresswomen Mimi Walters of California and Elise Stefanik of New York.[6] The morning before the meeting, I called a friend who worked with a conservative activist group. He got the word out. Radio shows, blogs, and social media lit up about the move to oust me.

The House leadership was inundated with angry callers, and the leadership must have known that some members were stepping up to defend me as well. By that evening, Majority Leader McCarthy told the freshmen leading the recall effort to back off. On Thursday morning, we did have the freshman meeting, and I wasn't in control of it. Mimi Walters and Elise Stefanik ran the meeting. Instead of removing me as they had originally planned, they gave each freshman member a chance to critique my performance. They knew they didn't have the votes to do anything, so the meeting ended with no change in leadership. During the meeting we agreed not to speak with the press about what transpired; I abided by that, but I noticed others didn't.

Still, the beltway bullies had suffered at least a temporary defeat because the American people had spoken.

CHAPTER 6

CORPORATE WELFARE

"The Party seeks power entirely for its own sake. We are not interested in the good of others; we are interested solely in power, pure power."

—George Orwell, *1984*

The battle over the TPA rule signaled the beginning of the end for John Boehner as Speaker of the House. It wasn't only the blatant retaliation that riled so many; it was the petty punishments too.

After opposing Boehner for Speaker, for example, Congressman Mark Meadows of North Carolina found his ability to advance causes he cared about seriously diminished. He was initially asked to serve on the new anti-Semitism caucus, because of his strong support for Israel, and was nominated to be one of the representatives on the Helsinki Commission, which monitors human rights in Europe. Congressional leadership cancelled both opportunities because Meadows wouldn't play their game.

Many members of Congress went along with the bullying *because* they wanted to retain their positions on committees where they thought they could do good work. But I thought that was a bad bargain. The Republican leadership under Boehner wanted your voting card and your money, and if you sold out to them I wasn't sure how much real good you could possibly do. A congressman is supposed to represent his constituents, vote his conscience, and defend the Constitution, not go along and get along with the rulers of the swamp.

Meadows put forward a motion to vacate the office of the Speaker—essentially, to fire John Boehner. His resolution cited what he viewed as Boehner's most egregious offenses, among them: Boehner had consolidated his own power, often bypassed the members and punished those who disagreed with him, and stood idly by while the executive branch trampled upon the authority of Congress.

The Rules Committee could ignore the motion—and they did, but it gave voice to the growing Republican opposition to Boehner and his methods.

Over the 2015 August recess, many members heard from angry constituents who weren't happy with Boehner's leadership of the House. Boehner knew his position was unsustainable. On September 25, 2015, he announced he was resigning as Speaker and leaving Congress by the end of October.

But he had one more initiative up his sleeve before he left.

"A SLUSH FUND FOR CORPORATE WELFARE"

The Export-Import Bank of the United States is supposed to encourage American exports by making low-interest loans, but it's really no more than a corporate welfare program.

The Ex-Im Bank began in the midst of the Great Depression in 1934 with an executive order by President Franklin D. Roosevelt. It was later approved by Congress as an agency following World War

II and played a pivotal role in helping Europe and the USSR rebuild. But that was seventy years ago. Today it is a lobbyist's playground.

I actually agreed with then-Senator Barack Obama when he called the Ex-Im Bank "little more than a slush fund for corporate welfare" in 2008.[1] But that was before he ascended to the White House. He also said American exporters should compete on quality and price rather than with government-subsidized financing.

After he opposed the Bank in 2008, Obama praised its expansion in 2012 and 2014. Then he joined forces with the departing Boehner to push for renewing its charter in 2016. It just so happened that the company that received the most Ex-Im Bank funding was a major Obama donor:

> Boeing Co. donated $1 million to this year's [2013] inauguration festivities for President Barack Obama, making it the third-largest corporate donor nationwide.... At Mr. Obama's first inaugural celebration, contributions were limited to $50,000 and no corporate donations were allowed.[2]

Apparently, things changed when Obama was no longer accountable to the people. Dan Holler of Heritage Action bluntly describes Boeing's taxpayer-funded benefits:

> In the banking industry, the U.S. Export-Import Bank is commonly referred to as Boeing's Bank. And it's not hyperbole. While the taxpayer-backed Bank claims nearly 80-percent of its loan guarantees go towards small businesses, the overwhelming majority of the total dollar amount goes to Boeing. By some estimates, the massive multinational

aeronautical company receives upwards of 80-percent of the Ex-Im Bank's taxpayer-backed loan guarantees.[3]

Of the financial guarantees made by the Ex-Im Bank in the 2015 fiscal year, Boeing received more than 70 percent—$5.5 billion.[4] In 2013, $90 billion of the bank's $112 billion portfolio went to just ten multinational companies, with Boeing at the top of the list. In fact, in both 2007 and 2013, well over half of all benefits went to only five companies. Boeing once again led a list that included General Electric, Applied Materials Inc., and Bechtel Power in both years.[5] And yet Boehner, Obama, and other bank supporters claimed the entity was essential for supporting small business.

The facts disagreed.

More than 81 percent of the 2013 funding went to big business.[6] The Heritage Foundation's Diane Katz, a research fellow in regulatory policy, demonstrates that those who gain the most are what she calls "monster corporations" like these:

- Boeing, the world's largest aerospace company, with a market cap exceeding $91 billion
- General Electric, the appliance and lighting conglomerate, valued at $267 billion
- Dow Chemical Co., the materials and chemicals producer, with 2013 sales of $57 billion
- Bechtel, the engineering and construction transnational, ranked by Forbes as the fourth-largest privately held company (by revenue)
- Caterpillar, global purveyor of mining and construction equipment, with 2013 sales and revenues of $55 billion

- John Deere, the king of tractors and dump trucks, ranked 97th on the Forbes 500[7]

The Bank itself claims it fills the gap for American businesses "when private sector lenders are unable or unwilling to provide financing.... Because it is backed by the full faith and credit of the United States, Ex-Im assumes credit and country risks that the private sector is unable or unwilling to accept."[8] Yet the Bank's leader, Fred Hochberg, said, "Big commercial jet makers like Boeing tend to arrange their own financing."[9] And the managing director of Boeing's financing department said he was confident the company could secure other funding sources if Congress did not reauthorize the Ex-Im Bank.[10]

So American taxpayers subsidize and assume the risks for loans that Boeing and others could easily secure on their own. When the bank loaned more than $27 billion in 2013,[11] we had a federal budget deficit of $680 billion.[12] We spent money we didn't have to do what didn't need to be done.

I have nothing against any of these companies, but they are *not* small businesses. To argue that the Ex-Im Bank's primary purpose is to help small business is simply disingenuous. According to Timothy P. Carney of the *Washington Examiner*, "The phrase 'small business' appears 101 times in the annual report and the word 'Boeing' doesn't appear a single time until you reach the back section, which lists all of the long-term loans and guarantees of the past fiscal year. There, Boeing appears 20 times."[13] Nevertheless, Ex-Im Bank Chairman Fred Hochberg claimed his organization "can help small businesses take the financial risk out of exporting products and services."

Meanwhile Boeing is selling more than eighty planes to the largest state sponsor of terrorism—Iran—in a deal worth more than $25 billion, and efforts to stop the deal in the House were called "unpatriotic."[14]

My friend Senator Mike Lee called the bank "a breeding ground for cronyism and for corruption."[15] My colleague Ohio Republican Congressman Jim Jordan summed up the case against the Ex-Im Bank this way:

> Every time the bank is up for reauthorization, deep-pocketed special interests and their well-heeled friends on K Street descend on Washington with Chicken Little fables about how small businesses across America will suffer if the bank's charter is allowed to expire. The reality is that the bank is to corporate welfare what the "bridge to nowhere" was to earmarks. Programs such as the Ex-Im Bank are exactly what the American people hate about Washington. They let government bureaucrats pick winners and losers, doling out taxpayer-funded handouts to well-connected corporations.[16]

IT ONLY GETS WORSE

The Ex-Im Bank is one of those instances where the corruption is not only immoral or unethical, but often downright illegal. Bribery, corruption, and fraud—throughout my tenure as a state and federal prosecutor, I saw all of these evils and more. I'm disappointed to say that the words I once used to describe white collar criminals can now be used to define a federally funded entity. The Ex-Im Bank has taken advantage of our free market system. An institution that once stood for economic growth, prosperity, and global expansion now stands as a symbol of greed, a pillar of crony capitalism.

This eighty-year-old institution we once trusted to expand our Made in America brand to every corner of the globe has failed to live up to its charter and has instead morphed into something else. The bank does not maintain or create jobs. It does not support small businesses as much as its supporters would like you to think. It does not level the playing field for U.S. exporters. And it is certainly not a good deal for taxpayers.

At best, the bank is handpicking winners and losers. At worst, Ex-Im Bank is accepting bribes, steering funds to favorite foreign companies, and killing the market for our homegrown companies.

Delta Airlines, an American company, sued the Ex-Im Bank because it believes it is being cheated out of airline routes. Foreign competitors—aided by American taxpayer funded loans from the Ex-Im Bank—can now charge less per flight because they purchase Boeing aircraft at cheaper prices than Delta and other American companies can. In other words, the American taxpayer is subsidizing foreign airlines that compete with American airlines. When Delta sued, Congress required the Bank to perform economic impact reviews on all large deals. Take one guess who helped Ex-Im craft these rules: Boeing—the very company that received the bulk of the Bank's financing to help sell their jets to foreign companies in the first place.

A quick glance at Ex-Im's leadership reveals how we got to this point. Fully half of Ex-Im's own advisory committee members led businesses or unions that directly benefited from Ex-Im financing during their term. Another five represented companies or unions who benefitted just prior to them joining the advisory committee.[17]

Most disturbing of all, the current advisory committee chair is former Democratic Governor Christine Gregoire of Washington state,[18] home of Boeing. Washington state companies received 43.6 percent of the bank's total funding from 2007 to 2014 and more than 22 percent of all exports from Washington state are backed by the Ex-Im Bank.

If this is not bad enough, between October 2007 and March 2014, there were 124 investigations linked to corruption surrounding the Ex-Im Bank. This includes some 792 separate claims involving more than $500 million. Nearly forty Ex-Im employees have already been investigated or are currently being investigated for fraud.

During an Oversight and Government Reform Committee meeting in the House, the Export Import Bank's inspector general revealed that four senior level Ex-Im employees had been relieved of their duties in 2014. These employees were allegedly steering taxpayer-funded loans to favorite companies in exchange for cash payments and other kickbacks.

One of them, a former Ex-Im loan officer named Johnny Gutierrez, was the first of the four to be formally charged with bribery by the Department of Justice. He allegedly accepted cash bribes nineteen times between 2006 and 2013 to help direct taxpayer-backed loans to a Florida-based construction equipment exporter, Impact Association. Apparently quite good at his job, he allegedly secured between $1 million and $5 million to finance Impact Association projects in both Mexico and the Dominican Republic in June 2007.

It only gets worse. In 2009, former Democratic Congressman William J. Jefferson from Louisiana was convicted for accepting bribes from U.S. telecom company iGate and a Nigerian company in exchange for selling access to Ex-Im Bank employees. Jefferson was even videotaped receiving $100,000 at the Ritz Carlton Hotel in Arlington. When federal investigators raided Jefferson's house, they discovered more than $90,000 in cash stashed away in his freezer.

Yet another Ex-Im employee, Maureen Scurry, was indicted for accepting $173,500 worth of bribes to help the Nigerian company.

Even the bank's own employees understand that something isn't right. An internal poll of the Ex-Im Bank employees showed that only 42.1 percent thought the organization's leader maintained a high standard of honesty and integrity, and only 50.2 percent believed they could disclose violations of the law without fear of losing their jobs.[19]

Clearly something was terribly wrong. Many members of Congress agreed with me that the Ex-Im Bank is the perfect example of what happens when the government is allowed to pick winners and losers. As Boehner tried to push approval through the House before leaving Congress, nearly half of the Republicans in the House joined me in opposing the bank's renewal. Not only was it no longer necessary, but it had become a breeding ground for greed and corruption.

When a bill to reauthorize the corrupt bank came to the Financial Services Committee, Chairman Jeb Hensarling voiced his opposition: "If we are ever, ever to deal with the threat of a social welfare state, we must first take care of the corporate welfare state. And the face of the corporate welfare state is the Export-Import Bank.[20]

DOUBLE STANDARD

As head of the Financial Services Committee, Hensarling blocked any further movement of the bill, steadfastly refusing to let the corrupt Ex-Im Bank waste more taxpayer money.

As a result, the bank's authority expired on June 30, 2015. And that should have been the end of it. If ever there were corruption Congress could reject, surely it would be the Ex-Im Bank. But yet again, the playground bullies in Congress sunk to new lows.

Boehner and his allies once again chose to make common cause with the Democrats, this time by using a discharge petition, which is normally never used when your party is in the majority. If signed by a majority of House members, a discharge petition can force any specific bill out of committee and onto the floor of the House for a vote. The only reason anyone in the majority party (in this case, the Republicans) would start one is if he or she intended to align with the minority party (in this case, the Democrats).

Yet that is exactly what Tennessee Republican Steven Fincher did. To his credit, Majority Leader Kevin McCarthy opposed the Ex-Im Bank reauthorization even though he was, at the time, widely assumed to be Boehner's heir apparent as Speaker.

The discharge petition was signed by a majority of the House members, mostly Democrats, forcing a vote in the House. A minority of Republicans (sixty-two) teamed up with a majority of Democrats (184) to force a vote over the objections of the vast majority of Republicans.[21] The next day, 127 Republicans joined with almost every Democrat to reauthorize the corrupt agency.

The bill eventually made its way back to the Senate and was signed into law by Obama on December 4, 2015. The *New York Times* trumpeted the vote as an act of "rare bipartisanship" as many Republicans who opposed the discharge petition voted for reauthorization—"but only once the bill's passage was assured."[22] Once again we saw that Washington works great, just not for the American people. The "bipartisanship" simply shoved us further into bankruptcy in order to promote special interests and expand the role of the federal government.

And what became of the member who initiated the discharge petition or the sixty-two Republicans who signed the petition to dump their own party for a chance to reauthorize the corrupt agency?

After seeing the consequences to those who voted against the TPA rule, one might think that those who tossed their own party under the bus with the Ex-Im Bank would face some stiff consequences.

But you would be wrong.

In a blatant display of the double standard that exists in Congress, there were no consequences for those who signed the discharge petition. Mark Meadows succinctly captured the lesson learned: "I guess the moral is that you can break the rules as long as the leadership gives a wink and a nod to break the rules when it supports something they want."[23] Not only did no one get punished, but the majority of financial support continued to flow to Republicans who played the game.

As for John Boehner, he left Congress and secured a $300,000-a-year role as director at R. J. Reynolds, a tobacco company that spent tens of millions in lobbying efforts while he served in House leadership.

CHAPTER 7

SWAMP-BASED ACCOUNTING

"A government big enough to give you everything you want is a government big enough to take from you everything you have."

—Gerald Ford

F rom 1939 to 1946 the national debt grew more than 600 percent, as the United States prepared for and then fought in the Second World War.[1] In inflation-adjusted dollars, the national debt was $3 trillion in 1946. That sounds like a lot until you realize that today the national debt is more than *$20 trillion.*[2] We could fight a world war in the 1940s and still only incur *one-seventh* of the debt our spendthrift federal government incurs today. That's incredible.

Our post-World War II debt maxed out at 113 percent of our economy. That means we owed more money than our entire nation could generate in one year. Again that sounds pretty bad until you realize that for the fiscal year ending in September 2016, our national debt equaled 107 percent of our economy.

Everyone can understand how and why we ran up a giant financial debt in World War II. What is harder to accept is how and why in a time of relative peace and prosperity, a cowardly Congress multiplied our national debt times seven purely in the interest of shameless vote-buying with government programs we can't afford but that congressmen think can ensure their reelection. It's been a gradual but inexorable process. Since the 1960s, money coming into the federal government has consistently ranged between 17 and 20 percent of the national Gross Domestic Product. But spending has ranged between 17 and 26 percent.[3] That difference adds up.

And it's not just a giant economic risk; it's a national security risk. In the late 1960s, foreign countries held less than 5 percent of our debt. Now they hold almost 50 percent. The nation holding 21 percent of that debt is China.[4] Communist China is not a friend of the United States. It is a direct military threat to our allies and our interests in the Pacific. But our options for responding to China's threats are limited by the reality that we owe China a lot of money.

HOW BUDGETS GET BUSTED

Even though the debt and deficit spending are such enormous threats to America's prosperity and power, under the leadership of Nancy Pelosi, Boehner, and others before them, the normal House budgeting process, which might have held congressmen more accountable, has been largely circumvented so that federal spending is determined not by the representatives of the people, but by a handful of powerful elites.

One in particular has emerged with extraordinary power to spend—the chair of the Appropriations Committee. During my first term it was Republican Congressman Hal Rogers of Kentucky. Called the "prince of pork" by the *Lexington Herald-Leader*,[5] Rogers has built quite the reputation for bringing federal funds home to his district throughout his thirty-seven years in Congress. It used to be that the Appropriations Committee is where the most conservative members of Congress would serve to ensure spending was kept in check. When Boehner chose Rogers to head up the powerful Appropriations Committee after Republicans regained control of the House in 2010, Rogers actually said, "The nation is in a fiscal crisis, and hard decisions are coming."[6] Seven years later, the crisis has worsened, and we're still waiting for Rogers and leaders of both parties to start making those hard decisions.

Here's how it works: when Congress passes a budget for the fiscal year, it doesn't actually spend any money. The budget simply sets the general boundaries on expenditures and establishes how much money can be spent and in what areas. The president has no authority in setting the budget, but he usually sends his own budget to Congress to try to frame the conversation.

Once the House and Senate agree on a budget, the real spending happens, or is supposed to happen, through twelve pieces of legislation known as appropriations bills. It is in this appropriations process that representatives of the people are supposed to have a say in how money is spent.

There are twelve appropriations subcommittees with budgetary jurisdiction over each of the twelve appropriations bills. The subcommittees hold hearings, set the spending numbers, and then send the bills to the full committee for approval before they go to the floor of the House. Or at least, that is how it is supposed to work.

However, the last time all twelve bills passed before the beginning of the fiscal year was in 1994.[7] When Congress fails to pass these bills, it creates a crisis, and the crisis creates an opportunity for corruption.

A crisis allows congressional leaders to threaten a government shut-down, or that America will plunge over a "fiscal cliff," if members don't approve spending bills written by the leadership and dumped on the members at the last minute.

That's *not* how it's supposed to work. According to the Constitu-tion, the House holds the power of the purse because the representa-tives have the most direct accountability to the American people. Crisis decision-making removes that accountability and leaves fiscal decisions in the hands of the elite few.

During John Boehner's tenure as Speaker, appropriations subcom-mittee members were expected to approve whatever expenditures the chair, Hal Rogers, sent their way. This is called the *chairman's mark*: the bill marked with the chair's spending wishes. When Republican Congresswoman Cynthia Lummis of Wyoming and Republican Congressman (now U.S. Senator) Jeff Flake of Arizona served on the Labor, Health and Human Services, and Education subcommittees for appropriations, they steadfastly refused to let bills out of the sub-committee unless they had an opportunity to reduce spending. Lead-ership repeatedly and publically castigated them for not blindly accepting the chairman's mark.

Nearly every time the Steering Committee met, Rogers would berate "those two members" who refused to endorse his personal spending decisions. Rogers labeled Lummis and Flake un-Republican and un-American. He said they were obstructionists and that no one voting against the chairman's mark should be allowed to serve on appropriations. He said on more than one occasion, "These people need to be punished."[8] Inevitably, Lummis and Flake had their con-gressional travel restricted. Lummis resigned her seat on the appro-priations subcommittee after only one term. Flake moved on to the

U.S. Senate. And the $1.1 trillion in discretionary spending has been left largely in the hands of the Republican leadership.

WELCOME TO BUDGET MADNESS

In 2010, when the Democrats controlled both houses of Congress, they didn't pass a budget or a single spending bill because they didn't want to be labeled as "big spenders" in the 2010 mid-terms.[9] That strategy didn't work too well, as Republicans made historic gains.

When Democrat Harry Reid led the Senate, the Democrats stopped passing a budget altogether. In 2015, with the Republicans now in charge, the Senate passed a budget for the first time in six years.[10] Over the last decade, however, the leaders of both parties have resorted to omnibus spending bills (that roll appropriations bills together with little oversight from the subcommittees) and continuing resolutions so that members can avoid making politically tough decisions.

Dr. Angelo M. Codevilla, author of *The Character of Nations*, calls omnibus spending bills "the greatest violation of popular government's norms—never mind the Constitution—to have occurred in two hundred years." Rolling government spending into one massive bill "eliminates elected officials' responsibility for any of the government's actions, and reduces them either to approving all that the government does without reservation, or the allegedly revolutionary, disloyal act of 'shutting down the government.'"[11]

Boehner had actually promised to restore the normal congressional budget process, but ditched that promise as soon as he realized that it meant open debate on contentious issues and tough votes with potential political consequences.

Even as Boehner was stepping down in the fall of 2015, he left one last fiscal mess for Congress. With only seven hours before the fiscal year expired on September 30, 2015, the House passed another continuing resolution to, once again, push the tough choices past the November elections. After the elections, the lame-duck session, which used to be reserved for emergency issues, has become the preferred time for Congress to make any unpopular budget decisions it has to make.[12]

Our founders intended for members to answer to the people for their votes. But when Congress plans the legislative calendar in order to avoid accountability, America has a problem. As former Congressman and Senator Jim DeMint has noted:

> Legislators who lose their seats in November, but vote on major bills in a lame duck [session], *have little incentive to please their constituents, and a bit more incentive to please Wall Street and K Street*. Ex-congressmen need jobs too— and they often get them on those particular thoroughfares.
>
> Even legislators who hold onto their seats know that a lame duck [session] is the perfect time to sneak through massive, big-government spending bills when most Americans have happily turned to family and football after election season.[13] [emphasis mine]

The new Speaker, Paul Ryan, has shut down a lot of the playground antics so common under Boehner's leadership. He has worked hard to move Congress in the direction of fiscal sanity. But he too has had to rely on continuing resolutions, in his case because of Democratic efforts to obstruct Republican-approved appropriations bills.

It will take more than a few good men like Paul Ryan to drain the swamp and reform Congress.

HOW BUDGETS GET MADE IN THE SWAMP

Congressional leaders call the budgets they approve *aspirational*, because they offer guidelines rather than hard caps on government spending. I call that *nonsense*. But it's also why Senate Democrats didn't pass a budget for six years—*because it didn't actually matter*. Spending would go on regardless.

A favorite congressional trick is passing a ten-year budget plan that front-loads expenses and backloads assumptions of higher revenue and lower deficits. Of course, congressional budget plans aren't binding on future Congresses—and the numbers never add up anyway. For example, the 2004 federal budget predicted a *surplus* of $518 billion by 2013. The federal government actually ran a *deficit* of $615 billion in 2013—a difference of more than $1 trillion.[14] The 2002 budget was even worse, predicting a $614 billion *surplus* by 2012. Actual spending in 2012 produced a *deficit* of more than $1 trillion— a difference of more than $1.6 trillion.[15]

How can this happen? It can happen pretty darn easily when *a third* of all discretionary spending is spent on programs *that Congress itself says we should not fund*. (I'll explain how that happens in the next chapter.) It also doesn't help that so much "mandatory" spending for entitlement programs—$2.1 trillion in fiscal year 2014—isn't even part of the appropriations process, it is simply on autopilot.[16] According- ing to the Congressional Budget Office, mandatory spending on entitlement programs is set to rise to $3.9 trillion within the next ten years.

From fiscal year 1962 to fiscal year 1975, mandatory spending jumped from a third to nearly half of the federal budget (45 percent). By fiscal year 2014, more than 60 percent of all federal spending was mandatory. Mandatory spending is simply a fast-track to bankruptcy, because it is spending that holds no one accountable. Congress should be forced to authorize and appropriate spending—not guidelines, but real spending caps—for every government program every year. That's what representative government and Congress's power of the purse is supposed to be about—exercising leadership, authority, and oversight on how taxpayer money is allocated.

Instead of doing that, Congress tries to deceive the American people with accounting gimmicks. Under the sequester bill of 2011 (the Budget Control Act), any spending increases have to be offset by additional government revenue, generated by taxes or sales of government property, or by other budget cuts. Congress calls these "pay-fors," and they can be slippery things.

For example, the House passed legislation known as the 21st Century Cures Act in 2015. The legislation would have increased spending dramatically for the National Institute for Health (NIH) and benefited big pharma companies and medical equipment manufacturers. Not surprisingly, Republican Congressman Fred Upton of Michigan, the primary sponsor of the act, was "the top recipient of contributions from the pharma industry in 2013–14" and serves as the chair of the Energy and Commerce Committee.[17] *Forbes* writer Judy Stone sums up the pay-for scenario for the bill:

> In addition to annual increases of at least an additional
> $1.75 billion per year, the bill promises an additional $2
> billion per year for five years to create an "NIH Innovation

Fund." Funding would come from "revenue generated from the sale of SPR [Strategic Petroleum Reserves] oil."[18]

Thanks to the growth of domestic petroleum, we're no longer as dependent on foreign oil suppliers as we once were. So the decision to sell some of the reserves *could* have merit, except the oil was sold for a substantial loss.

> The Energy Department, which oversees the reserve, says on average the U.S. paid about $29.70 a barrel for the oil. But after adjusting for inflation and other items, the average cost rises to $74 a barrel, according to ClearView Energy Partners, a Washington-based energy research firm. On Tuesday, West Texas Intermediate, the U.S. oil benchmark, traded at less than $44 a barrel.[19]

That's a net loss of at least thirty dollars per barrel—a 40 percent loss—to justify a spending increase elsewhere. What sane person would call that a wise financial decision? Yet these are the practices congressional leaders use to *pretend* as if they're saving money.

Democrats made matters worse in this case by insisting on making the new spending for NIH mandatory, so that long after revenue dries up from the oil sale, America still has to keep paying for the legislation. Moderate Republicans eventually caved and agreed to make this new spending mandatory. The legislation stalled in the Senate and failed to pass in 2016 before finally being amended and passed by Congress in late 2016.

But the same antics get used elsewhere and often. And the same pay-for can be used more than once. For example, expected revenue from the sale of strategic oil reserves did double duty in fiscal year

2016, allegedly offsetting two increases rather than one.[20] And it was used yet again to cover a gap in the Highway Trust Fund in a transportation bill.[21]

Anywhere else in America, that practice would be called fraud. When executives at Enron tried it, they went to prison. The reason congressional leadership can get away with using pay-fors so loosely is that no one keeps track of these supposed cuts and revenue increases. When Congress claims it will crack down on Medicare fraud to generate another $10 billion, no one is responsible for verifying that this actually happens.

The ten-year budget for the fiscal years 2017–2026 assumes $7.9 trillion in "savings" via pay-fors, including $2 trillion in savings from repealing Obamacare, $1.5 trillion from "mandatory program reforms," $1 trillion from "block granting and capping Medicaid," $579 billion from cutting "war-spending" to zero after 2021, and $449 billion from "Medicare policy changes." All of these might be laudable reforms, but we have no way of knowing, right now, whether they will happen at all, let alone how much such reforms might cut costs in the budget. Cracking down on fraud and reforming programs sounds great—it's often used to "offset" additional spending—but the numbers are all imaginary and they are never checked against reality. Even when cuts are supposed to be automatic, we have no assurance that cuts are actually made; and the Government Accountability Office (GOA) reports that in some cases, federal agencies that experience an automatic cut in one year get the money back in later years.[22]

That's swamp-based accounting.

CHAPTER 8

ZOMBIE GOVERNMENT

"No government ever voluntarily reduces itself in size. Government programs, once launched, never disappear."

—Ronald Reagan

G overnment programs are often the living dead.

Here's an example. In 1973, the Endangered Species Act became law, and the northern spotted owl was listed as a potentially endangered species. The federal government limited logging and lumber production in the Pacific Northwest to protect the owls' habitat.[1]

The result, over the intervening decades, was economic devastation for the logging industry in the area, and, ironically, no improvement in the fate of the spotted owl, whose numbers have continued to decline—not because of renegade loggers but because the eastern barred owl has pushed the northern spotted owl aside. So, in short, the program was another bureaucratic boondoggle that cost private sector jobs, devastating the local logging industry, and wasting taxpayer dollars. But maybe the worst part of the story is this: authorization for the Endangered Species Act expired on September 30, 1992.[2] Yet Congress keeps spending money on it. It's one of many government programs that simply will not die.

SUNSET PROVISIONS

The original Endangered Species Act (ESA), and a 1988 amendment to it, contained a sunset clause. A sunset clause functions like an automatic shut-off for legislation and federal programs. After some period of time, usually five years, the legislation or program expires *unless* Congress reauthorizes it.

Sine 1835, Congress has kept the authorization of government programs separate from appropriating money for them in order to ensure that Congress carefully reviews government spending. Unfortunately, in recent decades it hasn't worked out that way. Sunset provisions, which require that a program be reauthorized *before* any additional funding can be appropriated for it, are routinely ignored. In fiscal year 1989, about 8 percent of all federal spending was unauthorized by Congress. That seems high until we realize that in fiscal year 2016, 27 percent of the discretionary spending was unauthorized. More than $310 billion was appropriated in 2016 through the omnibus spending bill *without* authorization, which means *most* nondefense discretionary spending for fiscal year 2016 was unauthorized.[3]

Keep in mind that Congress spent this $310 billion on unauthorized programs in the same year that it ran a deficit of $590 billion. Unauthorized programs accounted for more than half of the budget deficit in fiscal year 2016.

Not all of the unauthorized programs should be shut down. Some of them are good and necessary and should be reauthorized. Incredibly, Congress has failed to reauthorize, but continues to spend money on, the State Department (since 2003), the Federal Elections Commission (1981),[4] the Federal Trade Commission (1998), National Weather Service (1993), the Federal Bureau of Investigation, the Drug Enforcement Agency, and the Bureau of Alcohol, Tobacco, and Firearms (all since 2009). The Congressional Budget Office also identified numerous programs such as the National Aeronautics and Space Administration (NASA for $19 billion in 2016) and the National Institute of Health ($31 billion for 2016) as part of the 256 laws that were funded in 2016 even though they were expired.

A lot of the unauthorized spending could be eliminated, or at least significantly trimmed, without disrupting the security and well-being of our nation. However, when Congress doesn't provide oversight—as the American people elected their representatives to do—no one knows which ones should be continued and which should be permitted to vanish.

CONGRESSIONAL COWARDICE

So why don't members of Congress do what they were elected to do? Why don't they use the constitutional power of the purse? In a word, *character*.

Reauthorizing legislation means members must go on record as either supporting or opposing a bill or program. When those votes could effect reelection chances, doing nothing starts looking like a pretty good option—if self-interest is the highest priority. It also works another way. Legislation that would never otherwise pass Congress can gain approval and eventually become law because rather than voting no on a program that has a special interest behind it, members will approve the program to please the special interest while telling opponents not to worry because the program will expire in five years.

It's one of the many ways members of Congress have their cake and eat it too.

The existing rules in the House do not allow for unauthorized spending.[5] Yet the Speaker of the House has the final say in how these rules are applied and whether or not they are enforced. Consequently, the Speaker can choose to ignore the wisdom of our founders and let funding continue without accountability, and that is exactly what often happened under Pelosi and Boehner. House rules grant members the right to object to unauthorized expenditure as a point of order, but congressional leadership has eliminated that right on appropriations bills in recent years.

What we're left with in the House is fire-alarm oversight. Congress often waits for something to go wrong *before* investigating to see whether a program should be funded. The omnibus budgeting process—or budgeting by crisis instead of by regular order—simply enables reckless, unauthorized spending. After all, when there are only days or even hours to review spending bills passed down from the chair of Appropriations and party leadership, there can be no careful review of programs and legislation. Spending levels either get kicked down the road *as is* or automatically increased in the panic to "get something done."

Although the courts have ruled the maneuver to be technically legal, it is both unwise and unethical for Congress to spend money on unauthorized programs and legislation. The Constitution grants the House the power of the purse for a reason. It is the branch of government most accountable to the American people. Only the House can start the process of spending money. It is yet another dereliction of duty for House leadership to continue spending on unauthorized programs.

WINKING AT WASTE

Because of Congress's lack of oversight, taxpayers are wasting a lot of money on unauthorized programs. The waste in the Endangered Species Act, for instance, isn't limited to the spotted owl program. The act has proven to be so ineffective that only slightly more than one percent of the species added to the list have ever recovered enough to come off of it. If we were truly serious about environmental protection, surely we could come up with a more effective program—and one that, unlike the current act, doesn't punish private citizens with endless regulations and lawsuits.[6]

Or consider the fiscal white elephant that is Obamacare. Its authorization expired in 2014.

Thanks to a lack of government oversight, the National Science Foundation, which had its authorization expire in 2013, continues to fund ludicrous studies on everything from the dating patterns of unattractive people, to evaluating the effectiveness of tweets ($2.6 million), and the social interactions of guppies. They also managed to find $1.2 million to build a life-size version of the arcade game Pac-man.[7] In a year when our national debt jumped by $1.4 trillion, you might think we had other spending priorities.[8]

Even when the House investigates and finds fraud, as it has done at the National Institute of Standards and Technology, which had its authorization expire in 2013, it continues to be funded.[9] One NIST laboratory was even apparently the site of an illegal meth lab. The lab was discovered only when it exploded.[10] And still the money flows, including to the National Endowment for the Humanities and the even more wasteful National Endowment for the Arts, which has found money to digitalize "classic" lesbian, gay, bisexual, and transsexual films, as well as promote the opening of a play about gun-control activist lesbians (do you sense a theme?), and a puppet show about cows learning how to type.[11]

As with the Endangered Species Act, some programs are on auto-pilot even though they are, by any measure, failures. Head Start is a prime example. Its authorization expired in 2012, and while it received more than $9 billion in funding in 2016, a study done by the Department of Health and Human Services, which administers Head Start, found that the program had little or no impact or even a *negative* impact on the kids who participated in it. Since its inception, the failed program has cost taxpayers more than $180 billion. Yet Congress keeps funding it.[12]

These wasteful programs, and legions of others, are often referred to as "zombie appropriations" because they stagger forward undeterred by anything, confident they will receive funding regardless of performance.

SUE AND SETTLE

The waste is bad enough, but these programs are also tools of bureaucratic harassment. Nowhere is this abuse more clearly seen than in the use of the "sue and settle" process. Once popular during President Bill Clinton's administration, it was revived under President Obama. Here's how it works in the hands of bureaucrats wielding the Endangered Species Act.

First, environmental groups file a petition to add a new species or sub-species to the threatened or endangered lists. Then those same groups sue the Fish and Wildlife Service or similar agencies, claiming the agencies have failed to protect a specific species and demanding action be taken by a certain date. Agency officials then meet behind closed doors with the group's leaders to negotiate a settlement.

The truth is the agencies often want to take the action anyways, but need a way to do it without public scrutiny. These negotiations are not open to the public, a clear violation of the 1946 Administrative Procedures Act, which ensures public participation in the creation of rules by regulators. The agencies essentially agree with whatever the group wants—because they wanted the same thing. Finally, the judge issues a consent decree making the agreement the law of the land—all without Congress and the American people having had any say in the matter.

More than 512 such suits were filed against federal environmental agencies between 2009 and 2016.[13] Between 2009 and 2013, the government agencies settled more than seventy such deals in this way.[14] Those settlements resulted in more than one hundred new regulations and an additional $100 million in annual compliance costs.[15]

The Center for Biological Diversity (CBD), and other groups such as WildEarth Guardians were at the center of a massive 2011 settlement that affected the listing of more than 700 species. When sued by these groups, the U.S. Fish and Wildlife Service agreed to the settlement that included taking action to protect the lesser prairie chicken whose habitat covers several states.

Just to the southeast of the district I represent in Colorado, Oklahoma Attorney General Scott Pruitt filed suit in 2014, claiming the EPA was colluding with environmental groups to advance an anti-energy agenda, not to practice sound science. He accused the agency of violating the law by sidestepping the rule-making process.[16]

Two years later, the Obama administration dropped its effort to list the chicken as "endangered" after the judge ruled the agency had ignored more than $26 million in conservation efforts already undertaken by several states and businesses. Undeterred, the CBD filed yet another lawsuit in August 2016 seeking action on more than 400 other petitions.[17]

The sue-and-settle process abuses the purpose of the ESA and creates havoc for the American people. But it also makes a lot of money for environmental groups. Taxpayers paid the suing groups' legal fees in forty-nine of seventy-one cases settled between 2009 and 2013.[18]

Incredibly, and conveniently for those environmental groups, the federal government does not track the specifics of how much it pays and whom it pays for those legal costs. In some cases, names of attorneys and groups are even redacted from records for alleged privacy concerns. Under the unauthorized Endangered Species Act alone, however, taxpayers have paid out more the $30 million in attorney fees since 2009.[19]

It's a shakedown racket. Groups such as the Sierra Club and the Center for Biological Diversity flood the agencies with petitions to list every conceivable species. They set arbitrary and artificial deadlines for the agency to respond. Then they sue the agency when it doesn't meet their timelines. And the settlements begin.

All of this corruption is made possible by the lack of congressional oversight that comes from legislation not going through the normal reauthorization process.

OBLIGATED TO ACT

I'm not the first member of Congress to sound the alarm over unauthorized spending. In 2013, Republican Congressman Tom McClintock of California sent a letter to Speaker Boehner calling for a return to regular order and an end to circumventing the process:

The first step in that process—and the most important—
is when programs are authorized or re-authorized: legislation must first be adopted that establishes the programs for
which money is subsequently appropriated.

This is an absolutely critical function that assures federal programs are constantly being scrutinized and that
Congress is asking: are these programs effective? Are they
meeting their goals? Are they worthwhile? Are they worth
the money we're paying? Most programs have time limits
on them to assure that these questions are periodically
asked.

The legal authorization is the green light to the appropriations committee to provide funding for that program.[20]

During orientation in the Republican conference meeting in 2014,
McClintock made a motion to change the rules to require authorization once again. Only a small handful of us voted for the rule change.

Speaker Boehner did nothing to force reauthorizations. His actions
were consistent with his desire to protect his majority from difficult
votes. Speaker Ryan has shown a commitment to restoring regular
order, but he faces an uphill battle against a culture intent on preserving
the status quo and avoiding hard decisions. Speaker Ryan introduced
his new plan "A Better Way: Our Vision for a Confident America." It
calls for requiring the chairs of authorizing committees to review and
make recommendations on how to best deal with these unauthorized
programs. But it is only a suggestion and not likely to generate a lot of
enthusiasm from politicians trying to dodge tough votes.

Still, it's a start; and if voters make it an issue, maybe we can gain
some momentum with it in Congress.

CHAPTER 9

PROFITEERING IN THE SWAMP

"The question before the House is one of awful moment to this country. For my own part, I consider it as nothing less than a question of freedom or slavery."

—Patrick Henry

W hat if I told you executive branch agencies raised $516 billion in user fees, fines, and settlements in 2015 with no oversight from Congress? Would you believe it? It's true. According to the Office of Budget and Management, federal agencies collected more than half a trillion dollars in addition to the money Congress appropriated for them.

That's the equivalent of one sixth of the entire federal budget and almost one half of the entire discretionary federal budget amount. The agencies collected $516 billion in fees in a fiscal year when the American people saw Congress run a budget deficit of $439 billion.

Congress had nothing to say about where that money went, because the truth is we don't know where it went. By failing to fulfill its responsibility to provide accountability and oversight, Congress has created a for-profit government, in which agencies are incentivized to generate more revenue for themselves. The more they can charge the American people, the more money they have to spend. Congress manages to keep its hands clean of the whole affair with a shrug of its legislative shoulders.

BUREAUCRACIES GONE WILD

Under the Constitution, Congress has oversight of every dollar the government collects and spends. Article I, Section 7 specifies that, "All bills for raising revenue shall originate in the House of Representatives." Article I, Section 8 states that, "The Congress shall have power to lay and collect taxes, duties, imposts and excises, to pay the debts and provide for the common defense and general welfare of the United States."

But over time, and especially in the last few decades, Congress has delegated authority to executive branch agencies to collect fines and fees for permits, licenses, and regulatory approvals. But they've chosen to remain silent as to where that money goes or how it is used. Consequently, executive agencies effectively tax the American people without any credible oversight by their representatives.

The U. S. Government Accountability Office (GAO) actually gives these entities a name only a government agency could concoct: Non-Appropriated Fund Instrumentalities (NAFIs). In other words, they collect and use money outside of the normal appropriations process. They are managed by federal employees and answer only to themselves. No one even knows how many of these NAFI entities exist or how they spend their funds.[1] In 2016, Professor Michael Greve of the George Mason University Antonin Scalia Law School and lawyer and research fellow Christopher DeMuth found that "Neither the Office of Management and Budget, the Department of the Treasury, the enforcement agencies, nor Congress publishes (or, as far as we know, even compiles) systematic accounts of agency revenue-raising and the uses made of the funds."[2]

When most Americans visit a national park and pay a fee, or purchase a boating license for use in federal waters, they assume they are doing their patriotic duty. But the fact is Congress already appropriates money to run the national parks; these extra charges or fees or even fines are leveled by the agency and can be spent however it wishes without congressional oversight.

As expected, this lack of accountability often leads to abuse. The small businessperson often feels the pain the most. A local greenhouse grower told me that when the Occupational Safety and Health Administration inspected his facilities, they fined him $5,000 for not having a spec sheet for a bottle of Windex used to clean bathroom mirrors. They then offered to settle the claim for "only" $500.

On the other end of the scale of abuse, the National Oceanic and Atmospheric Administration (NOAA) used fishing fines that can reach six figures to buy a thirty-five-foot boat for $300,000. Supposedly the boat was purchased to "monitor whether whale watch boats in Washington's Puget Sound were harassing the animals." But the reality was quite different. The boat was only used nine times in several years, all for pleasure—making trips to restaurants and hosting parties that included alcohol and non-federal employees.[3]

The NOAA also used fines to fund conferences in exotic locations, hosting government contractors and the judges who approved the fines that financed the NOAA "conferences."[4] In one egregious case, a fisherman lost his home, which had been in his family for 350 years, and when an inspector general investigated the NOAA, its chief of law enforcement shredded most of the documents related to the case. Instead of being fired for his action, he was actually considered for a promotion.[5]

It would be polite to call this a hidden tax. It is corruption pure and simple. The list of abuses is seemingly endless. The Department of Agriculture tried imposing a fee on Christmas trees, and when that resulted in bad publicity, levied a "marketing fee" on almost every other agricultural commodity.[6] The Department of Energy collected fees for thirty years for a nuclear waste disposal facility that didn't exist[7]—for a total of more than $30 billion.[8]

Often Congress itself doesn't realize that all these fees and charges mean that the agencies really aren't all that dependent on appropriations. When talk of a government shutdown surfaced in 2013, the Department of Homeland Security contingency report revealed that a shutdown would have little impact on its ability to function, largely because so much of its funding came from sources other than Congress. The U.S. Citizenship and Immigration Services, for instance, relied on fees for nearly 95 percent of its annual budget.[9] All told about 86 percent of the Department of Homeland Security's employees would remain on the job, even in the event of Congress appropriating no money during a government shutdown.

THE ASSET FORFEITURE FALLOUT

Another great boon for the agencies is asset forfeiture. Asset forfeiture started innocently enough in 1984 with the passage of the Comprehensive Crime Control Act. The intent was to strengthen law enforcement efforts, especially in the war on drugs, by allowing agencies to keep property seized in investigations. Soon Department of Justice agencies started stockpiling money in an Asset Forfeiture Fund outside the purview of Congress.

In 1992, the power expanded to include Treasury Department agencies, such as the IRS. At that time, Congress decided to prioritize law enforcement, giving "exclusive and perpetual control" of forfeiture funds to the Justice and Treasury Departments.[10] Two unintended consequences occurred. First, billions of dollars began to accumulate for use by these agencies outside of congressional oversight. Second, law enforcement agencies in general now had a "profit incentive." The more property they seized, the more they might benefit.

Carole Hinders, owner of Mrs. Lady's Mexican Food in Spirit Lake, Iowa, had nearly $33,000 seized by the IRS from her cash-only restaurant in August 2013. The IRS claimed this grandmother had intentionally avoided federal reporting requirements for large transactions by making numerous smaller transactions, a practice called "structuring." After fifteen months and a lawsuit, the IRS finally decided *not* to press charges and returned her money nearly two years later. However a motion to have her attorney fees reimbursed was denied.[11]

Lyndon McLellan, a North Carolina convenience store owner, had more than $100,000 seized by the IRS on similar charges. It took him over a year to get his money back, and another lengthy lawsuit before the IRS was required by a federal judge to reimburse him for more than $20,000 in legal fees.[12] Unfortunately, there are plenty of similar stories. The IRS seized nearly $250 million on "structuring" accusations between 2005 and 2012 alone. On average, the IRS keeps wrongfully collected money for at least a year before it returns it.[13]

Instead of working to fix this unjust system of bureaucratic self-enrichment, Congress has cashed in. In both the 2013 and 2015 Bipartisan Budget Acts, Congress withdrew a combined $2.3 billion from the Asset Forfeiture Fund accounts to pay for more spending elsewhere. That's how things work in the swamp. Congress creates a problem, and then makes it worse.

CLINTON CASH

She might have lost the 2016 presidential election, but Hillary Clinton epitomizes the self-centered corruption that typifies life in the Washington swamp. The accounts of her scandals have filled many books, yet she continues to prosper from her shady dealings in Washington, as if above the law. As a former prosecutor, I was disappointed by the FBI's investigation into Clinton's mishandling of classified documents when she was secretary of state. She used an unprotected personal email server to send and receive clearly marked, classified information. Then she denied knowing what the classification markings meant and repeatedly obstructed the investigation. Based on the FBI's own findings, Clinton was clearly guilty of gross negligence, yet she faced no charges. If you or I had done even a little of what the FBI claims she did, we would be in prison—guaranteed.

There is ample evidence that she used her position as secretary of state to her financial benefit, as well. The Clinton Foundation was begun by Hillary's husband, former President Bill Clinton, and has raised more than $2 billion since 2001. Donations from foreign governments were not always fully disclosed during her tenure as secretary of state. Algeria, for example, donated $500,000 to the foundation while it was seeking to develop a closer relationship with Washington. According to the *Washington Post*, donations with suspicious political connections are common for the Clinton Foundation:

> [M]any of the foundation's biggest donors are foreigners who are legally barred from giving to U.S. political candidates. A third of foundation donors who have given more than $1 million are foreign governments or other entities based outside the United States, and foreign donors make

up more than half of those who have given more than $5 million.[14]

As emails leaked last year show, friends of Bill Clinton were given special treatment and access to the State Department while his wife was in charge:

> In a series of candid email exchanges with top Clinton Foundation officials during the hours after the massive 2010 Haiti earthquake, a senior aide to Secretary of State Hillary Clinton repeatedly gave special attention to those identified by the abbreviations "FOB" (friends of Bill Clinton) or "WJC VIPs" (William Jefferson Clinton VIPs).[15]

Other emails reveal similar access for foreign nationals who made substantial donations to the foundation. One of those donors was a Lebanese billionaire with ties to criminal activities in Nigeria.[16] As Peter Schweizer, author of *Clinton Cash* puts it, "What these emails show is that it was not a coincidence, that the Clinton Foundation was a conduit for foreign oligarchs basically to gain access to the highest levels of the State Department."[17]

Both Bill and Hillary Clinton have spent their entire political lives surrounded by scandal. President Bill Clinton was even impeached and disbarred. I don't need to go over the litany of scandals here. There are plenty of excellent books on the subject.[18] But what is telling is that all these scandals did nothing to stop Bill and Hillary Clinton from being celebrated by the Democratic Party and the swamp beasts of Washington. That should tell you something.

VIGILANT, ACTIVE, AND BRAVE

The corruption is not just about money, it is about lives. In November 2016, an American Special Operations soldier became our first combat casualty in Syria. His commander-in-chief had sent him there, and he had done so without authorization from Congress.

Following the terrorist attacks of September 11, 2001, Congress authorized the president to use military force against Al-Qaeda in Afghanistan and later in Iraq. It has never authorized military intervention in Syria. According to our Constitution, Congress alone has the authority to declare war. President Obama never asked for congressional approval to send troops to Syria. More important, Congress didn't demand that he do so. It's impossible to enforce the laws of the land when the president, the Congress, and the courts won't follow the law—and that's frequently been the case in recent years.

Draining the swamp won't happen if left to Congress alone. It will require brave, vigilant, and active Americans who require their representatives in Congress to do what they have been elected to do.

CHAPTER 10

WHEN WASHINGTON TAKES CONTROL

"This country has gotten where it is in spite of politics, not by the aid of it. That we have carried as much political bunk as we have and still survived shows we are a super nation."

—Will Rogers

"Let's call ourselves 'problem-solvers.'"

That's what a ranking member of Republican leadership told me and about twenty other Republican congressmen in a closed-door strategy session. I thought it was one of the dumbest things I'd ever heard. We had gathered to hear pollster Frank Luntz tell us what words and phrases were resonating with voters; one of them was *problem-solvers*. So the Republican leadership encouraged us to describe ourselves that way. *Call me crazy*, I thought, *but what if instead of calling ourselves problem-solvers, we actually got busy solving problems?*

PROBLEM-MAKERS

Also, to my mind, they got things backwards. Washington isn't in the business of solving problems, it creates problems; and when bureaucrats or congressmen think they're in the business of solving problems—rather than executing their constitutional duties—they inevitably make them worse.

A good example is the Department of Education. The federal government's role in education is supposed to be small—education is a state and local responsibility—and when the federal Department of Education was founded in 1979 by President Jimmy Carter, its first secretary, Shirley Hufstedler, a former judge, pledged to reduce regulatory red tape. She claimed the department would not supersede local control or attempt to impose restrictive regulations.[1] The purpose of the department, we were told, was to help local schools by promoting the best "success models."

As we know, that hasn't worked out so well, as American education has taken a nose dive, especially since the founding of the Department of Education. In 1990, the National Governors Association, responding to warnings that American education was getting so bad that it represented "a nation at risk," set the goal of making American students first in international test scores in math and science, improving scores in all basic subjects, and achieving a high school completion rate of 90 percent.

Today, with the help of the federal Department of Education we spend twice as much per student as we did thirty years ago and our students rank forty-eighth in the world in math and science, high school graduation rates are at 70 percent, and 76 percent of high school graduates are not academically prepared for first-year college courses.[2]

That's a typical performance by Washington "problem-solvers." And blame belongs to both parties. President Ronald Reagan, to his credit, wanted to eliminate the Department of Education, but he quickly realized that it was politically impossible because Congress did not want to appear *anti-education*.

Republican President George W. Bush took education spending to a whole new level by signing the No Child Left Behind (NCLB) Act in January 2002. It gave Washington even more control over our nation's schools. The legislation was authored by Democratic senator, and big-government hero, Ted Kennedy of Massachusetts and a lesser-known House Education committee chairman named John Boehner. Boehner later called NCLB the "proudest achievement" of his political career. Little wonder, then, that I witnessed him resorting to his usual tactics to preserve his legislative legacy in 2015.

Authorization for NCLB had expired in 2007, but of course it just kept rolling along. When Boehner tried to officially reauthorize it in February of 2015, he didn't have Republican votes and had to pull the bill from the House floor in a series of embarrassing missteps. When the bill returned in July, Boehner and the Republican leadership agreed to let Republican Congressman Mark Walker of North Carolina offer an amendment that would let states opt out of the unproductive legislation. Those states could then determine their own curriculum and spending priorities without interference from the federal government. Walker could only offer his amendment, they said, if he could first produce a list of conservative members who would promise to vote for the NCLB reauthorization. Walker did just that. He secured the required number of votes for the legislation based on leadership's commitment to offer his amendment.

When the amendment came to the floor, however, Boehner and friends actively whipped *against* Walker's amendment, twisting arms and pressuring members to defeat it. They convinced enough Republicans to join all the Democrats to keep the states from opting out of federal intrusion. Boehner won by one vote.[3] Then they used Walker's list of Republican members committed to voting for the bill to get the reauthorization passed.

Education is not the only area where a federal program or department was created with promises of reform only to become more expensive mud for the swamp. After the 2015 August recess, the Republican leadership began laying the groundwork for a massive transportation bill. It's a good thing I wear cowboy boots with my suit, because it sure got deep. We heard repeatedly about how disgraceful it was that transportation funding involved thirty-six short term extensions over ten years and how we have an aging system of roads, bridges, and transit systems. The best argument big spenders could use with a Republican base was that this proposed bill would reform the transportation system. As if on cue, the newspapers and TV stations began to transmit the reform message to my constituents back home.

The message from Republicans and Democrats alike conveniently ignored the fact that the Highway Trust Fund had required $73 billion in bailouts over the past seven years. As I explained to my constituents, the Highway Trust Fund is now used to fund a lot more than highways, including local transit projects, bike paths, and museums. I quoted Peter Drucker in town hall meetings when I explained why we really don't want more federal control over transportation:

It is reasonably certain that we would still have stagecoaches—nationalized, to be sure, heavily subsidized, and with a fantastic research program to "retrain the horse" —had there been ministers of transportation around 1825.[4]

In early November 2015, the House passed the Surface Transportation Reauthorization and Reform Act (STRR). I got a good sense of transportation priorities when the House voted against an amendment keeping Highway Trust Fund money from going to landscape projects.

What happened next was bizarre even by congressional standards. The House passed a six-year bill that authorized spending of $325 billion. The Senate countered with a transportation bill that authorized $342 billion over six years. A Conference Committee convened to hammer out a compromise between the two bills called the Fixing America's Surface Transportation Act (FAST). The Conference Committee's compromise bill called for more money being spent over a shorter period of time than either bill originally suggested. As the Heritage Foundation noted:

> The outcome represents a caricature of congressional negotiations: one chamber proposes an unsustainable spending bill, the other proposes even more spending, and they "negotiate" a level even higher.... The FAST Act claims to reprioritize federal spending on federally-relevant projects, but in the same breath brags about increasing support for local bus programs by 89%.[5]

Hailed as another major bipartisan achievement, the House voted 359 to 65 in favor of the FAST Act Conference Report, paving the road to bipartisan bankruptcy.

THE TRANSPORTATION TRAFFIC JAM

Truckers try to avoid driving through the Rocky Mountains. They often take I-80 through Wyoming and then head south on I-25 into Denver, which puts a lot of truck traffic on an interstate that has only two lanes in both directions.

Several years ago, there were two efforts to help alleviate the traffic jams on I-25. The federal government wanted to widen I-25. The local authorities decided a better alternative was widening Weld County Road 49 (WCR 49), which runs parallel to I-25. Not surprisingly, the local project has come in at a third of the cost of the federal project and is practically done and already relieving traffic. The federal project has barely started, delayed and burdened by $20 million in federal environmental impact studies (which local authorities can skip if they don't use federal funds), Davis-Bacon wage laws, and other federal regulations.

These Davis-Bacon Act (DBA) wage laws came about during the Great Depression, more than eighty years ago. Today, about sixty federal laws require the use of DBA wages. Based on these laws, all federal contractors must pay the "going rate" for contractors doing similar work in their region. But that rate is determined, not by state and local officials, but by the Department of Labor (DOL) in Washington. The DOL also sets the minimum amount of fringe benefits that all employees working on federal construction contracts must receive. In other words, contractors can't compete to deliver the best work at the lowest rate. Washington bureaucrats set the wage rate and benefit levels. The burden falls on contractors to figure out how to classify each worker in accordance with the bureaucratic standards or face stiff penalties. These outdated laws dramatically increase the costs associated with every federal construction project.

Washington wasn't supposed to be in control of our highways and interstate system. When President Eisenhower signed the Federal-Aid Highway Act of 1956, popularly known as the National Interstate and Defense Highways Act, it contained a provision to return control to the states. The federal gas tax that funded 90 percent of the initial build was also to revert to the states for maintenance. But like so many other sunset law provisions, it never happened. Because Washington never surrendered control—of the money and the roads—now every federal transportation project takes longer and costs more.

Even worse, Congress has used the money collected in the Highway Trust Fund on all sorts of other non-highway projects, such as light rail, buses, and streetcars. At least 25 percent of the federal fuel tax is now spent on non-highway projects.[6] In 2014, $8 billion of that fuel tax was spent on mass transit projects—not highway projects—and another $820 million on transportation alternative projects such as sidewalks, bike paths, highway beautification, and recreational trails. Largely because of these new additions, the Highway Trust Fund has been running deficits in recent years. Congress has had to bail the fund out to the tune of more than $73 billion since 2008.

As an example of how the highway system is used for pork barrel politics, Times Square became an arterial route to the national highway system in 2012 so New York City could receive additional money from the Highway Trust Fund. New York City got indigestion on all that pork, however, when it discovered it wouldn't get $90 million in additional funding because the iconic neon billboards violated the 1965 Highway Beautification Act that limits signs to being no larger than 1,200 square feet.[7] New York City is now attempting to receive an exemption from the U.S. Department of Transportation.[8] My question is why are local roads in New York City getting any money from the national Highway Trust Fund?

We could actually maintain our highway system with the Highway Trust Fund if Congress didn't routinely divert the money for other projects, such as helping out New York City or providing for "highway beautification," a federal program that, typically, started small with Lady Bird Johnson championing the sowing of wildflowers along highways in the 1960s, and eventually morphed into all manner of projects that have little to no connection with maintaining our nation's highways.

Now in order to keep the highway fund solvent, Congress has resorted to more than thirty "short-term" patches to the fund since 2009, while making no cuts to spending.[9] In 2015, the proposed patch used fees imposed on airline passengers by the Transportation Security Administration (TSA) to fund surface road spending.[10] This particular patch violated the House's own rule, known as CUTGO, which requires Congress to offset mandatory spending with comparable cuts.

The federal government needs to get out of the interstate highway business and turn that authority over to the states, as was supposed to happen decades ago. The result would be better roads or roads at a more affordable price, with fewer pork barrel projects, and more local control.

Congress is reluctant to do that, because Congress loves the power. Part of that power comes from the public misperception that our national infrastructure is crumbling. It simply isn't true. Study after study has confirmed the same thing: we need regular maintenance, not massive upgrades. For example, the percentage of bridges requiring significant repairs has declined from 22 percent in 1992 to only 10 percent in 2014.[11] Washington doesn't need more money for infrastructure projects. That's just an invitation to more corruption.

The control and maintenance of infrastructure projects should be given to the states.

THE DEPARTMENT OF ANTI-ENERGY

The Department of Energy was created in 1977 in response to the Arab oil embargo. The expressed purpose of the department was to reduce American dependence on foreign oil. Forty years later, America would be just as dependent on foreign oil if private innovation hadn't bypassed the Department of Energy's efforts. All the federal government accomplished was to spend your money to delay our progress towards energy independence.

Thanks to improved hydraulic fracturing (fracking) technology—which pumps pressurized water, sand, and chemicals underground to break open oil and gas deposits—America is more secure and has more energy resources than we thought possible even a decade ago. Washington bureaucrats and ideologues have opposed this new technology every step of the way.

For example, the Environmental Protection Agency (EPA) blamed foul-smelling water it discovered in 2011 near a drilling site in Pavillion, Wyoming, on fracking. Scaremongering like this was used in an attempt to discourage fracking projects. But when the Wyoming Department of Environmental Quality finished its detailed investigation, it found that the EPA had done a bad job of drilling its test wells, introducing artificial materials into the water, and that these had clogged screens at the bottom of the wells, where the standing water had become stagnant and a breeding ground for stinky bacteria. Fracking had nothing to do with it.[12] As is so often the case, the government intervened where there was no problem and created one.[13]

Ronald Reagan once wryly noted that the nine most terrifying words in the English language were, "I'm from the government, and I'm here to help."[14] He was right. We shouldn't look to the federal government for help. Instead, we should demand that the federal government be trimmed down to size by our elected representatives so that our states, our local authorities, and we the people can have more power over our own lives, and the federal government less.

We need to get back to a basic understanding of what the Constitution requires of our federal government. The federal government is supposed to be small. Its power is supposed to be limited. The United States is supposed to be a union of largely sovereign states. The Constitution would never have been ratified had there not been agreement to include a number of amendments including the Tenth Amendment, which states:

> The powers not delegated to the United States by the Constitution, nor prohibited by it to the States, are reserved to the States respectively, or to the people.

Our founders' default position was to keep power as far from Washington as possible. We can no longer afford to ignore their wisdom. Our crippling national debt exists because Washington has too much power. Corruption in the federal government is a direct result of so many people getting comfortable in the stagnant political backwaters beside the Potomac. The concentration of power in D.C. attracts the worst and tempts the best, making it extremely difficult for men and women of character to arise and lead our nation to a healthier place.

The best way to drain the swamp in Washington is to remove the incentive for abuse. Swamps exist when water congregates in one place and becomes stagnant over time. Draining the swamp means draining Washington of power.

Washington can't abuse power it does not have.

THE SPREADING SWAMP

When President Lincoln founded the Department of Agriculture, it had one employee for every 227,000 farms. Today the ratio is one bureaucrat for every sixteen farms.[15] In America today, government employees outnumber those in manufacturing nearly 2:1.[16] And government work pays—with higher salaries and much better benefits than comparable private sector jobs.[17] The Washington, D.C. area is now home to seven of the nation's most affluent counties.[18]

Federal employees are not the only ones doing well in D.C. So are lobbyists. Between 2007 and 2012, the most politically active corporations in the nation spent a combined $5.8 billion on federal lobbying and campaign contributions. An analysis by the Sunlight Foundation revealed that those corporations received more than $4.4 trillion in government contracts and financial support from the federal government. Those 200 companies accounted for 26 percent of the total money spent on lobbying. The study found that "on average, for every dollar spent on influencing politics, the nation's most politically active corporations received $760 from the government. The $4.4 trillion total represents two-thirds of the $6.5 trillion that individual taxpayers paid into the federal treasury."[19]

If Washington didn't have all this power, we wouldn't have this problem.

WASTING AWAY IN WASHINGTON

The great irony of Washington's power-hungry ways is this: the more money and power those in Washington have, the less good they do. The problem manifests itself in two primary ways: waste and obstruction.

Often money simply gets wasted, lost in the bureaucratic maze of special interests. Back in the 1980s, Ronald Reagan famously highlighted the problem of waste in government by citing examples such as a $900 hammer for the Defense Department. The same problem is alive and well today in the Washington swamp.

Here are merely a few examples of how taxpayer money gets wasted when Washington has too much control:

- The Bureau of Indian Education schools teach 48,000 students at a cost 56 percent higher than the national average. Those schools have some of the lowest tests scores and graduation rates in the nation[20]
- The federal government has forty-two duplicative programs to provide non-emergency medical transportation[21]
- Log Lane Village in Colorado was forced to purchase new signs for the entire town after new federal regulations decreed that traffic signs could not be written in all capital letters. The town's total population is under 1,000[22]
- The National School Lunch Program made $1.8 billion in improper payments in fiscal year 2015. Medicaid made improper payments 10 percent of the time in fiscal year 2015, amounting to $29.1 billion. Unemployment insurance also had a 1 percent improper payment rate, which cost taxpayers $3.5 billion[23]

- A Veterans Administration (VA) hospital in Aurora, Colorado, was projected to cost $604 million. After mismanaging the project and repeatedly changing the specifications, the VA now projects it to cost more than $1.7 billion[24]
- The federal government spends more than $1.7 billion every year to maintain empty buildings. An audit of federal properties revealed that they were inaccurately reported about 88 percent of the time. Many properties being reported as *utilized* are actually *vacant*[25]

GETTING IN THE WAY

Not only does the federal government wantonly waste money, it often delays and obstructs necessary local projects.

I live in one of the fastest-growing counties in America. Like a lot of growing communities, we have water-supply issues. The problem isn't *lack* of water—we have plenty of water in Colorado—the question is how it is allocated. A lot of it is devoted to farms and a lot of it is allowed to flow out of state.[26]

About sixteen years ago, several communities banded together to work on the Northern Integrated Supply Project. The idea was to construct a reservoir to collect water they legally own. They purchased a 1,000-acre property for the project. Unfortunately for them, the property contained five acres with reeds—*wetlands*. Enter: the federal government.

The project leaders filed the appropriate applications with the federal government—and the agency roulette began. The Army Corps of Engineers, the Environmental Protection Agency, the Bureau of Reclamation—you name it, they all got involved in some way, often making conflicting demands, but all of them costing money, whether in environmental consulting, attorney, or architectural fees.

After fourteen years, the good people of Colorado still don't have a water solution. They are still negotiating with the federal government to get permission to build the reservoir even though the federal government's only interest is a five-acre piece of land it designated as *wetlands*. The Army Corps of Engineers doesn't expect to issue a Decision of Record until 2018. The United States of America rebuilt our entire Navy in eighteen months after Pearl Harbor, but it's taking eighteen years to even begin to build one water reservoir thanks to obstruction from Washington.

A similar story unfolded just south of Denver with the expansion of the Chatfield Reservoir. When local authorities decided to raise the capacity of the reservoir by twelve feet, the federal government stepped in. The reservoir is not on federal land. The federal government doesn't own the water. And yet it took more than fifteen years to get approval from the Army Corps of Engineers to raise the water level in the reservoir.[27]

The Audubon Society promptly sued to halt progress. Meanwhile, farms have dried up. Environmentalists claim they want to make sure no endangered species are being displaced, but the environmental damage from defunct farmland far exceeds any other possible harm to species that might exist in the affected areas.

Likewise, it's taken nearly thirty years to get one road approved in San Francisco thanks to environmentalist objections and bureaucratic headaches. The Presidio Parkway has seen its projected costs skyrocket from $600 million to over $1.4 billion with no clear end in sight.[28] The Army Corps of Engineers has been front and center in that fiasco, as well.

The American people deserve better. We don't need more Washington involvement in our lives. We need less so we can actually get things done. In the chapters that follow I'll show you how we can do that.

CHAPTER 11

HOW PRESIDENT TRUMP CAN HELP DRAIN THE SWAMP

"It's time to drain the swamp in Washington, D.C."

—Donald J. Trump

The superintendent of a public school in my district once called my office to call attention to a serious issue. Apparently, the children in his school were throwing away most of their lunches.

His school was required to comply with the Healthy, Hunger-Free Kids Act of 2010, spearheaded by Michelle Obama. Passed in a lame-duck session of Congress after Democrats lost the House to Republicans, the legislation revised federal lunch and breakfast programs for public schools. Part of Michelle Obama's Let's Move initiative, the law attempted to deal with the epidemic of child obesity by doing what Washington does best—throwing money and regulations at a problem. The law set vague guidelines, authorized more spending (of course), and empowered the Department of Agriculture (USDA) to create regulations for school cafeterias. Taxpayers were paying for it, but the kids weren't eating it.

The frustrated administrator told me that USDA regulations micromanaged the sodium, sugar, and whole-grain levels to such an extent that food offered to the kids was bland and unappetizing. They simply didn't like it. They preferred to go without eating than to eat what his school had to serve them. As a result, students were hungrier and eating more junk food—exactly the opposite of the law's intended effect.

I decided to visit another school in a rural part of my district to see first-hand what was happening. My rural district is hit particularly hard by these programs because these schools really struggle to get and keep good teachers, let alone pay for lunch programs. They have little margin for waste as they stretch limited resources to the max. After I ate lunch there myself, I saw the garbage container was half full of wasted food.

I'm sure every parent, every American, would rather that kids ate better and that we didn't have a problem with childhood obesity. But the federal government is not the way to address that problem. We used to have enough common sense to know that. But now it is too easy to grandstand and say that you don't care about kids unless you agree that the federal government—*the federal government*!—should be regulating the lunches in your local school and that taxpayers all across the country should be paying for school lunches that kids won't eat. When Washington regulates the American people to death, which it does all the time, the only ones who benefit are the bureaucrats who gain power and bigger budgets and the politicians who get to brag about how they spent money "on kids" or on whatever other apparently worthy cause they're spending money on. That's how the Washington swamp got built, through deals like that. If we're going to drain the swamp, we need to do the reverse. We need to take power *away* from Washington and return it to *the people*.

President Donald Trump campaigned on the slogan of "Drain the swamp!" and there's reason to think he can. But my hope is not in any one person. My hope is in the American people. President Trump will succeed in draining the swamp to the extent that he restores power to the people and authority to the states and local government.

As I know from sad experience, it will not be easy. But there are five things President Trump can do now to help drain the swamp.

1. RECOGNIZE THE LIMITS OF PRESIDENTIAL POWER

My first suggestion would be that President Trump rely *less* on executive orders and presidential directives—as he has pledged to do—than Barack Obama did. We need to restore the presidency to its proper constitutional role; and as we've seen, what was enacted by presidential decree can be undone by presidential decree. Real, lasting reform will come through legislative action and constitutional amendments that restrict federal power.

The founders never expected either the federal government in general or the president in particular to have anything like the power they wield now. The whole purpose of the Constitution was to establish an effective federal government *that would not trample on the rights of the states or the people*. The entire system of federalism and checks and balances was designed to this end, and when the federal government oversteps its boundaries, or the president takes on the role of *the legislative and* the executive branch, or when the president *chooses* which laws the executive branch will enforce and which it will ignore (and the Obama administration was guilty of both these things: legislating from the White House and selectively enforcing our laws), our liberties are threatened. As the great political philosopher Montesquieu warned, "There can be no liberty where the legislative and executive powers are united in the same person."[1]

It is also dangerous when the executive branch takes archaic legislation, badly in need of updating, as a tactical measure to undermine the rights of the states and the people. In February 2015, for example, President Barack Obama declared, citing the authority of the Antiquities Act of 1906, more than 21,000 acres of Colorado land in Browns Canyon as a national monument. Should that land have been set aside for conservation reasons? Maybe, but that was not the president's call. It should have been decided by state leaders, Congress, and the federal government working together, as they had done in the past. For instance, in 2009, a bipartisan effort of state, local, and congressional leaders worked together to designate 250,000 acres of wilderness in Rocky Mountain National Park. That's how our federalist, representative democracy is supposed to work. We are not supposed to be governed by presidential decree—or what separates a president from a king?

In his last months in office, President Obama locked up more than 125 million acres off the coast of Alaska declaring it "indefinitely off limits for future oil and gas leasing."[2] He did so using another outdated law, the 1953 Outer Continental Shelf Lands Act; and he did so without involving Congress or the people of Alaska or the incoming administration in his decision. Maybe even worse, the Obama administration claimed the presidential decree could not be undone because there was no expiration date on the ban. Talk about undemocratic.

Still, President Trump can, justifiably, and with the stroke of a pen, undo many of President Obama's swamp-protecting abuses of power. For instance, he could repeal executive orders that are essentially federal subsidies for "renewable energy" boondoggles,[3] repeal the several anti-Second Amendment executive orders issued by the president,[4] rescind the executive order that boosted the minimum wage for federal contractors,[5] close the gates thrown open by Obama to undocumented "refugees,"[6] and on and on and on. Federal overreach that can't be withdrawn by repealing an executive order, or by legislative action, can be defunded through congressional action. The Republican Congress, with Trump's encouragement and example, needs to take responsibility for this.

2. REIN IN THE ADMINISTRATIVE STATE

The expansive federal bureaucracy is often referred to as the fourth branch of government. But it shouldn't be; it needs to be trimmed. It wasn't just executive orders that the Obama administration abused, it was an avalanche of rules, regulations, and notices cranked out by unelected bureaucrats.

In 2016, Congress passed about seventy laws. But that same year *93,000* pages (as listed in the *Federal Registry*) of new federal regulations were enacted by the bureaucracy. That was a record. The previous record, also held by the Obama administration, was 81,405 pages, set in 2010. In fact, seven of the top ten years for federal regulations occurred during Obama's presidency. Bad laws can beget even worse regulations. The Affordable Care Act (Obamacare) itself ran for thousands of pages, but the federal regulations that have followed in its wake are running well over 10,000 pages (in the tiniest font) and they will keep running until the act is repealed.[7] The Affordable Care Act has been amended seventy times, and those amendments themselves are responsible for more than 11,000 new regulations resulting from the seventy changes alone. This is the sort of stuff the denizens of the Washington swamp feed on.

Trump can start draining the swamp by directing his administrative heads to follow through on his campaign promise of repealing two or three regulations for every new one enacted. He could also ask Congress to make this directive law and prohibit the creation of new "government charted entities," which is government speak for bureaucracies. President Reagan used a similar approach to great success during his own presidency.

Burdensome regulations are great for bureaucrats in Washington, but they are terrible for the economy. Federal regulations have reduced economic growth by about 2 percent each year for the last sixty-five years, according to some analysts.[8] It's been estimated that in 2012 alone federal regulations cost our economy more than $2 trillion.

Congress can, and likely will, roll back some of the most recent rules and regulations using the Congressional Review Act. The act gives Congress sixty legislative days to pass a joint resolution of disapproval of a final agency rule. If both chambers pass the resolution and the president signs it, the rule is overturned. However, the Senate must allow up to ten hours of debate per rule, which means that it's not an effective way to repeal regulations.

A better way is needed. The REINS Act would require congressional approval *before* significant rules move forward. The House passed this legislation again in January of 2017. President Trump has said he would sign it, and he should.

3. REPEAL AND REPLACE OBAMACARE

By the time you read this, Obamacare might have already been repealed. I certainly hope so. Obamacare represents all that is wrong with Washington. Obamacare was concocted behind closed doors without public debate by special interest groups, rammed through Congress using obscure legislative rules and procedures, massaged by big-business lobbyists to protect their interests over those of small businesses, passed only with the help of bribes and kickbacks, and supported solely by the Democratic Party. Not one Republican voted for it. It is one of the most unpopular laws ever passed in America, and the effects have been disastrous for our economy and the health of many Americans.

My first suggestion is that President Trump insist that the process used to repeal and replace Obamacare be driven by free and open debate. Instead of last-minute revelations with thousands of pages rammed through Congress, the new course of action should be debated well in advance of any votes. Let's not just get something done, let's get it done right.

Obamacare is so intentionally convoluted that repealing and replacing it will be an arduous task, but it should be guided by the principle of increasing competition to deliver the best health care possible, including:

- Letting insurers compete across state lines
- Making insurance more portable so that you can carry it from one job to the next—or into your own business. Auto insurance isn't tied to your job, which is why there is more competition among insurers and lower prices; we should do the same for health insurance
- Increasing the incentives, and providing tax credits, for people to use their own Health Savings and Flexible Savings accounts, which give people more control over their health care options

- Finding creative ways to keep the few popular elements of Obamacare. Even a blind squirrel finds an acorn occasionally. For example, we should find a way to provide a path for coverage for people with pre-existing medical conditions
- Reforming medical liability laws. Trial lawyers are one of the largest lobbying groups in Congress. The current system is designed to protect their interests and adds more than $300 billion in additional costs. The new plan should establish reasonable limits and not drive our best doctors out of medicine due to exorbitant malpractice insurance premiums
- Protecting and preserving Medicare. Obamacare attempted to raid Medicare for funds. The new plan should protect Medicare while reforming it so that it can be a sustainable program

4. RAISE REFORM ISSUES

President Trump campaigned on a five-point ethics reform plan. It's a good place to start. Here's what he said he would do:

1. Re-institute, through Congress, a five-year ban on all executive branch officials lobbying the government.
2. Ask Congress to institute a five-year ban on lobbying by former members of Congress and their staffs.
3. Expand the definition of lobbyist so that former government workers can't get around the lobbying ban by claiming to be "consultants" or "advisors."
4. Impose a lifetime ban against senior executive branch officials lobbying on behalf of a foreign government.

5. Ask Congress to pass a campaign finance reform law that prevents registered foreign lobbyists from raising money in American elections.[9]

President Trump has also said he will push for congressional term limits—another highly effective way to help drain the swamp. Being in Congress should not be a career; it should be a limited term of public service.

5. RESIST THE URGE TO BUY POWER

Candidate Trump said he could pay off the national debt in eight years. He later walked back that claim and suggested he could balance the budget in eight years.[10] He has excellent budget hawks on his staff—like his budget director Mick Mulvaney, who was part of the House Freedom Caucus—to help him do it. But like any politician he will tempted to spend—in his case on massive infrastructure projects that could easily become boondoggles. He needs to be resolute in balancing the budget. His experience as a businessman might help.

Trump is a dealmaker, but he needs to be careful with what Congress might do to his tax reform initiatives. Congressmen looking for campaign contributions are easy pickings for lobbyists. Nick Penniman, executive director of Issue One, a nonpartisan advocacy group that works on democracy issues, describes what needs to happen:

You'd think it would be common sense that if you go to Capitol Hill and lobby for or against a bill or a program, that you should be prohibited from slipping money into a member's pocket for reelection. Your case should stand on its own and that's what we are working towards—elevating the value of bold ideas, not just checkbooks.

Issue One has proposed prohibiting lobbyists from making donations for three months after lobbying a congressman or congressional staff member.[11] That's another reform Trump might want to support.

President Trump is a brash, frank, and outspoken man. If he insists on transparency from Congress; if he shines a light on how Congress actually does its business; he can send a lot of the swamp creatures skittering away, and he can encourage the American people to pursue the sort of lasting congressional reform that I've outlined in this book. In his first days in office President Trump instituted a hiring freeze on civilian federal workers. He noted that many federal workers are overpaid (and have better benefits) compared to workers who do similar work in the private sector.[12] He hinted that he intended to right this injustice to the taxpayers. He made clear his intention to slash unnecessary federal regulation. And he said that he planned to cut the federal budget by more than ten trillion dollars over the next ten years. These are all steps in the right direction. It's my job—and the job of every conservative in this country—to make sure he follows through.

CHAPTER 12

USING THE CONSTITUTION TO DRAIN THE SWAMP

"Our Nation's Founders gave us the means to amend the Constitution through action of state legislatures.... That is the only strategy that will work."

—Ronald Reagan

Congressional reform begins with stopping Congress from spending us into oblivion—and that begins with a balanced budget amendment to the Constitution. To make that happen I propose using a tool our founders gave us—the Article V amendment process.

Some of the founders themselves recognized the need for such an amendment. For example, Thomas Jefferson first proposed an amendment in 1798 to keep Congress from borrowing money. Twenty trillion dollars in debt later, we can understand why. On top of that, we need to put more limits on federal power, which can be done with the budget, and term limits on members of Congress. I propose these solutions as someone who has experienced Congress's business-as-usual corruption firsthand. I know they can work. And I know what won't work.

What won't work is expecting Congress to fix the problem on its own. Congress is not going to force itself to balance the federal budget and eliminate deficit spending, because the congressional leadership has little incentive to do so. We need to give them that incentive.

Congress came close to passing a balanced budget amendment as recently as 1995. Voters swept Republicans into a congressional majority in 1994 based on the Contract with America, which promised a vote on a Balanced Budget Amendment. The House passed the amendment easily. Fourteen Democrats joined with fifty-two Republicans in the Senate, but it wasn't enough. The amendment failed to clear the two-thirds requirement when Republican Senator Mark Hatfield sided with the remaining Democrats to defeat the effort *by one vote*.[1]

One vote would have sent the amendment to the states to be ratified. Polls showed an overwhelming majority of Americans favored the amendment. Looking back now at the trillions in debt we've accumulated since then, that was a pretty expensive vote. It was even closer than it looked. Some Democrats had said they would vote for the amendment if Congress were barred from dipping into the Social Security Trust Fund to balance the budget. The Senate couldn't agree to that.[2]

The first balanced budget amendment was proposed in Congress in 1936. In 1982, in the Reagan era, the Senate passed a Balanced Budget Amendment, but it failed to get the needed two-thirds approval in the House. And there are proposed balanced budget amendments in Congress right now, but they are going nowhere, because most congressmen think they get reelected by spending more. They will continue to do so until Americans make them stop.

WHY WE NEED A BALANCED BUDGET AMENDMENT

Forty-one states have some sort of balanced budget requirement; thirty-three of them are required to have balanced budgets by their state constitutions.[3] If the states can balance their budgets, so can the federal government.

At the simplest level, a balanced budget amendment would require Congress—and the president—to spend only the money actually received as revenue. With a balanced budget amendment in place, it would be illegal for the federal government to run an annual budget deficit except in extreme cases of war or national emergency, and then only with the approval of a supermajority in Congress. The president could not propose it, the House could not offer to do it, and the Senate could not approve it.

A balanced budget amendment would result in the following key benefits to the American people. It would:

- Restrict the ability of congressional leaders to manipulate the budget process for personal and political gain
- Lower the national debt
- Attract investment by improving America's bond rating
- Bolster the American dollar
- Free up credit, otherwise taken up by government borrowing, for job-creating private investment
- Stop the immoral burdening of our grandchildren with debt
- Force Congress to make the tough, but necessary, budget decisions it has been putting off for far too long—$20 trillion too long

A balanced budget amendment would force Congress to finally do its job of actually taking responsibility for the nation's finances. Agencies would come under closer scrutiny, because every dollar would matter. Government would be more responsible because it would be on a financial leash, and ineffective, wasteful, and unaffordable programs would have to go. And, as part of the balanced budget amendment, we would need to ensure that fees and fines are accounted for in the general budget—no more shadow budgets.

WRITTEN IN LETTERS OF GOLD

James Madison, in framing the Constitution with checks and balances, famously wrote, "Ambition must be made to fight ambition."[4] But he wasn't just writing about the executive, legislative, and judicial branches of the federal government. Our Constitution provides double security for the rights of the people through what Madison called the "compound republic of America."[5] Power in America is divided first between the national government and the states, and then subdivided amongst the branches of government at each level. This sharing of power between a central government and the many individual states is called federalism and lies at the heart of the Constitution. We sometimes forget that the founders saw America as "a sovereign nation of many sovereign states."[6]

While the rights of states have waned over the last century as the federal government has grown, the Constitution protects the right of the people to amend the Constitution through the states—and there is nothing Congress can do about it. Our founders wisely foresaw that if Washington became corrupt, no one in Washington would be motivated to do anything about it. Those living in the swamp would find it difficult to drain the swamp. So they gave the rest of us a way to amend the Constitution.

The way forward is found in Article V of the Constitution. Article V provides two ways for our Constitution to be amended.

The first way is the process used for each of the twenty-seven amendments to date. Two-thirds of both Houses of Congress can propose an amendment that then must be ratified by three-fourths of the states. Once ratified by the states, it becomes the law of the land. Article V provides another way to amend the Constitution, a way our founders believed critical to the long-term success of our nation. The states can require Congress to call a convention for the purpose of amending the Constitution to deal with specific issues:

> The Congress, whenever two thirds of both Houses shall deem it necessary, shall propose Amendments to this Constitution, or, on the Application of the Legislatures of two thirds of the several States, shall call a Convention for proposing Amendments, which, in either Case, shall be valid to all Intents and Purposes, as Part of this Constitution, when ratified by the Legislatures of three fourths of the several States, or by Conventions in three fourths thereof, as the one or the other Mode of Ratification may be proposed by the Congress....

In other words, if two-thirds of the states petition Congress to call a convention to propose constitutional amendments to address an issue, Congress has to do it. It is *not* optional.

The states may then vote to ratify any amendment that emerges from that convention, provided the amendments are aligned with the given reason for the convention in the first place.

If three-fourths of the states ratify the amendment, it becomes the law of the land. Congress can do nothing but abide by it.

The Constitution was ratified only because it contained this vital clause as a final protection of the rights of the states against the federal government. Colonel William Barton, a delegate to Rhode Island's ratifying convention, said of Article V: "This clause ought to be written in letters of gold!" He praised the Constitution, especially this "fair opportunity furnished for amendments provided by the states."[7]

Through Article V, our founders intentionally gave more power to the states. For Congress to amend the Constitution, both Houses must pass an amendment and then submit it to the states for approval. But the states do not need to get congressional approval for their amendments. Article V establishes the rights of two-thirds of the states to demand a convention, which Congress *must* call. The states can then approve the amendments that emerge from that convention and force Congress to comply.

Our founders gave more power to the states, because they recognized that self-interest and ambition could drive the federal government to exceed its boundaries. And they were right. We need to use this vital check on the power of the federal government.

HOW IT WORKS

Some have worried that a constitutional convention would become a "runaway" convention and dramatically change the Constitution. But that's not how it works. A constitutional convention is called for a specific purpose and it would only have authority to propose *amendments related to that stated purpose*. Even then, any amendments would need to be ratified by three-fourths of the states, hardly an easy accomplishment.

Supreme Court Justice Antonin Scalia noted that Article V was intended by the founders to serve as a popular check on Congress and the federal government:

> The founders inserted this alternative method of obtaining constitutional amendments because they knew the Congress would be unwilling to give attention to many issues the people are concerned with, particularly those involving restrictions on the federal government's own power.... The founders foresaw that and they provided the convention as a remedy.
>
> I do not have a lack of trust in the American people.... The people do not feel that their wishes are observed. They are heard but they are not heeded, particularly at the federal level.... The one remedy specifically provided for in the Constitution is the amendment process that bypasses Congress.[8]

On no issue is this more applicable that the need for a federal balanced budget amendment.

BALANCED BUDGET AMENDMENT BASICS

Here are some common sense elements any balanced budget amendment should have. First, it should require Congress to actually adopt a budget—on time, every year. Such a requirement used to be obvious until Congress stopped passing budgets all together. With no spending plan in place, economic chaos ensues.

Second, it would seem wise to have clear consequences should Congress and the president fail to do their duty. Automatic sequestration, or cutting of spending levels across the board, would force members concerned about constituents and special interests to get something done to avoid harsh consequences. A provision like this one puts teeth into the budget requirement so that politicians get bit where it hurts.

Third, a balanced budget amendment should include hard caps on spending so that expenses do not exceed income. Finally, although the balanced budget amendment should restrict Congress from borrowing money and counting it as revenue, there should be a provision by which Congress can take on short-term debt in the case of a national emergency or time of war. Based on the cowardice I have seen in Washington, such a vote should be on the record and require a two-thirds or even three-fourths majority.

A balanced budget amendment is not a magic bullet. Congress will certainly try to find ways around it, which is why an amendment will have to be written carefully to minimize such risks. But passing a balanced budget amendment is both an achievable and a necessary first step to draining the Washington swamp. It's time that all of us started accelerating our efforts to make it happen. In Appendix A of this book, you'll find an "Application for a Convention of the States under Article V of the Constitution of the United States." It's one of several efforts to make such a convention a reality. Together we can get it done.

CHAPTER 13

THROW THE BUMS OUT— AND OTHER REFORMS

"If I were only interested in advancing myself, I would only be a member of Congress, and I could focus on myself 100 percent of the time."

—Congresswoman Debbie Wasserman Schultz, former Democratic Party Chair

Being a member of Congress was never supposed to be a life-time employment. But for many, that's what it's become.[1] And even those who don't spend decades in Congress—the average member of Congress serves more than nine years—do the next best thing and often become lobbyists so they can keep paddling in the swamp.

President Trump supports, as do I, term limits for Congress to "clean up the corruption and special interest collusion in Washington, D.C.," as well as a five-year ban before members of the executive branch and members of Congress can be employed as lobbyists. Republican Senate Majority Leader Mitch McConnell, however, has declared that term-limit proposals are dead on arrival: "I would say we have term limits now," Mr. McConnell told reporters. "They're called elections. And it will not be on the agenda in the Senate."[2]

McConnell has been in the U.S. Senate for thirty-three years; he's the longest serving senator in the history of Kentucky.[3] He's about the last person you'd expect to want to drain the swamp, because he thrives in it, and you'd be right. He is a firm supporter of the Washington swamp status quo. And he's a perfect reason why we need term limits—because while his seniority might make him useful to some of the people of Kentucky, it also makes him a firm opponent of necessary congressional reform.

We need mandatory term limits in both houses of Congress. It might well require an amendment to the Constitution via the Article V process to get it done, because in spite of overwhelming public support for term limits, Congress has avoided taking action on it. Congressional term limits were actually part of the Contract with America, which propelled Republicans to a congressional majority in 1994—and still nothing happened.

RETURNING CONGRESS TO ITS PROPER ROLE

Mandatory term limits would refocus members on the reality that they are elected to serve, not to be served. In a free government, Benjamin Franklin noted, "the rulers are the servants and the people their superiors and sovereigns"—so much so that he believed that no one should be employed in government service for too long, because that would "keep them always in a State of servitude, and not allow them to become again one of the Masters."[4]

George Washington set the example of serving only two terms as our first president—an example that is now part of our constitutional law. But today most members of Congress and the federal government take a very different attitude.

In Franklin and Washington's day, there wasn't much incentive to stay in our nation's capitol, intentionally so. Members were paid six dollars for every day Congress was in session. Today, members of Congress receive an annual salary of $174,000, regardless of how many days we are in session.

In spite of what you might think from watching the 24/7 news cycle, Congress isn't actually in session all that much. For example, we were only scheduled to be in session for ten days in January, thirteen days in February, and ten days in March 2016. For the entire year, we were scheduled to work for only 111 days.[5]

But even those numbers are exaggerated. When we fly into Washington on a Monday, that day counts as a workday even though everyone understands little to no work will be done. Some members jokingly refer to them as "bed-check Mondays." Technically we have to be there, but we all know nothing of substance will take place. Likewise, the calendar says no votes after 3 PM on Fridays, but the halls of Congress are deserted by noon as everyone heads home. These calendar nuances mean we lose about a third of those 111 days to travel. Republican leadership in the House made a step in the right direction for 2017, scheduling the equivalent of three additional legislative weeks, but the light Mondays and Fridays continue.

I realize members have things to do in their individual districts, but this absentee pattern explains why so little gets done in Washington. It also gives undue power to the Washington staffs and congressional leadership. Even when in D.C., fundraising takes up a lot of time—up to half the day for some[6]—as members strive to meet dues requirements placed upon them by leadership.

I am not opposed to fundraising for the good of the party. I pay my dues to the National Republican Congressional Committee. Thankfully, I don't have to invest half my day into fundraising as some do, because in Colorado the congressional delegation hosts a few key fundraising events for a more efficient approach. The irony behind all this effort is that although members must raise more money to get plum committee assignments, they seldom use those assignments as intended because leadership consistently bypasses the regular order of the appropriations process. When leaders negotiate budget deals behind closed doors and roll all appropriations into omnibus bills or continuing resolutions, committees become irrelevant—and with them, the voice of the people goes silent.

I am not suggesting representatives should ignore their districts, of course, but making Monday a full workday would add nearly a month to the congressional calendar. More time in Washington means fewer excuses for budget crises and fewer excuses for not working on consensus bills for real reform—something that should be more achievable when members have a limited number of terms and are under pressure to get things done.

LET THE SUN SET

Another necessary step to draining the swamp is prohibiting Congress from spending money on unauthorized programs. These programs absorb about one-third of discretionary spending without genuine congressional oversight.

Republican Congressman Tom McClintock of California argued in a letter to Speaker Boehner in 2013 that authorizing committees should be given a year to authorize all programs or let those programs expire. His logic is tough to dispute:

If, after a full year, the authorizing committees don't believe the programs are worth the time to review, maybe that's just nature's way of warning us that they're also not worth the money that we continue to shovel at them.[7]

Boehner and the congressional leadership ignored McClintock's plea then. They ignored legislation in 2016, as well, from Washington Republican Congresswoman Cathy McMorris Rodgers. She proposed the Unauthorized Spending Accountability (USA) Act of 2016. The bill would have put responsibility on heads of federal programs to seek reauthorization. Programs that did not seek reauthorization would be penalized with mandatory, automatic spending cuts—10 percent the first year, 15 percent for the next two years, and then funding eliminated entirely after four years.

She rightly described the authorization problem as one that "prevents the American people from exercising their authority to review, to rethink, and perhaps eliminate government programs."[8] Her bill also would have empowered Congress to review all federal programs on a three-year authorization cycle and find savings in the process.

It was a good idea. She is a prominent member of Republican leadership. As the Republican Conference chair, she could have gotten the bill to the floor of the House with little opposition. But it went nowhere. The Majority Leader assigned it to the Budget Committee and the bill sat there for the remainder of the session.

The USA Act is a symbolic step in the right direction, but the fact that a ranking Republican leader proposed it—and it went nowhere, is more evidence that Congress is loath to do the right thing when the right thing is difficult to do. That's why an amendment like this—that would enforce sunset law provisions with automatic sequestration cuts—should be another goal of an Article V convention.

TAMING THE BUREAUCRACY

A balanced budget amendment to establish hard caps on spending, term limits to motivate and hold members accountable, and sunset provisions on all federal programs to force congressional review would do a lot to drain the congressional swamp. In addition, Congress needs to fulfill its constitutional role of providing a check to the power of the executive by its oversight of federal agencies and budgets.

John Locke, whose philosophy greatly influenced our founders' thinking, warned in his *Second Treatise of Government* that representatives of the people cannot delegate their authority to others. The people grant the legislative branch power to make laws, he said, not give authority to others to make laws. He warned, "The legislative [branch] can have no power to transfer their authority of making laws and place it in other hands."

The Unites States Supreme Court agreed in *Field v. Clark* (1982) stating that "Congress cannot delegate legislative power to the President is a principle universally recognized as vital to the integrity and maintenance of the system of government ordained by the Constitution."[9]

Yet that is exactly what Congress has done by permitting executive branch agencies to promulgate their own rules. These agencies make laws, but they do so outside the legislative process ordained by the Constitution. They then have to enforce the rules they make, which is why they require so much money.

Under a balanced budget amendment, Congress simply would not have enough money to pay for all their rules. Power would gradually revert back to Congress or to the states. But only if all funding sources are brought into the general treasury fund.

Congress must require executive agencies to funnel all receipts from fees, fines, proceeds, and settlements into the general fund of the treasury so that the power of the purse can be restored to the House of Representatives where it belongs. If agencies can fund their own missions, they won't need authorization or review from Congress. They will keep on functioning as a shadow government with shadow budgets.

To try to deal with the problem, Republican Congressman Gary Palmer of Alabama introduced the Agency Accountability Act in 2016, requiring all fines, fees, penalties, and other unappropriated funds collected by federal agencies to be transferred to the treasury, and subject to the appropriations process. This legislation would have gone a long way toward solving the problem. But after being introduced in June 2016, the Agency Accountability Act was referred to various subcommittees for review. Not surprisingly, it went nowhere.

Congress has a constitutional obligation to oversee the executive branch. If it doesn't, that might become just one more item to amend by the Article V process.

INSPECTORS GENERAL

Congress can improve its oversight of executive branch agencies by adjusting the role of the Office of Inspector General.

Inspectors general keep an eye on federal agencies and submit reports to Congress semi-annually. The 1978 Inspector General Act established twelve such offices. That number has now grown to more than seventy. Some inspectors general are nominated by the president and confirmed by the Senate; others are appointed by the head of the agency they supervise.

The problem with the current structure is that, although they submit reports to Congress, they owe their position to members of the executive branch. In addition, these inspectors general report to the heads of the agencies they inspect. The head of the agency determines his inspectors general budget and can thereby limit the extent of any oversight. Moreover, if an IG finds evidence of corruption in another agency, which sometimes happens, he has no power to do anything about it.

I believe that Congress should appoint inspectors general, with appointments requiring a two-thirds vote of both Houses to ensure bipartisanship. Congress should set their budgets. And inspectors general should report directly to Congress, not to the heads of the agencies they investigate. That seems like common sense—and a great incentive to reform, especially with a balanced budget amendment in place that will motivate Congress to eliminate agency waste, fraud, and abuse.

RESTORE REGULAR ORDER

Last September, the Senate voted to approve a spending bill that didn't even exist yet. According to our Constitution, all spending bills must originate in the House of Representatives. Yet Senate Majority Leader Mitch McConnell asked senators to sign on to a spending bill that might come their way later from the House. Maybe. Incredibly, the Senate approved the non-existent legislation eighty-nine to seven. The move reminded me of Nancy Pelosi's infamous claim that we needed to pass the Affordable Care Act to find out what was in it. Recently elected Republican Senator David Perdue of Georgia voiced his concerns about the bizarre move: "We've got a lot of work to do around here."[10] Indeed.

It is a simple fix, and Speaker Paul Ryan has promised to make it: we need to restore the regular House order. That means that House committees need to authorize, vet, and send legislation to the House floor in a timely fashion. We'll see if Speaker Ryan can make that happen.

DEVOLVE PROGRAMS TO THE STATES

Draining the swamp in Washington requires decreasing the power of the federal government and returning power to the states. Prime targets should be transportation and education, where the federal government has massively intruded on the prerogatives of state and local government with only huge bureaucracies to show for it.

Devolving power to the states means not only restoring the proper structure of our government, as the founders intended it. It means that we the people can better control how we want our money spent, what sort of infrastructure projects we want, and how we want to run our schools in the best interests of our children. The answers to these questions will surely be different in Alaska than they are in California and in Massachusetts and in Michigan. But that's the beauty of federalism. Every state can pursue its own path—and other states can take note when they see good examples of success in education or transportation or any other government project. The only thing that Washington brings to the table is red tape, delay, inflated budgets, bureaucratic central planning, special interests, and of course the bribery of federal funds, which are taxpayer dollars redirected from one state to another. That's a bad system—better that we get back to the federal system as the founders designed it.

I continue to hope that Congress, along with President Trump, will answer the call of the American people to drain the swamp—and act via the legislative process. But hope is not a strategy. Our founders gave us the Article V process for a reason. They intended for us to use it.

If our leaders will not act, it is the right and duty of the American people to do so. The Constitution, reproduced in toto in Appendix B, shows the way.

CHAPTER 14

WHAT YOU CAN DO TO DRAIN THE SWAMP

I met Al Wiederspahn when I worked in the Wyoming legislature and he was a Democratic state senator. We didn't always agree on policy, but we enjoyed many an evening talking politics, and I considered him a mentor.

An accomplished attorney, his hobby was refurbishing old buildings near Cheyenne, Wyoming, where he lived for many decades. He didn't do it for money, but to preserve our history, working with the National Trust for Historic Preservation.

Al was a talented and generous man. He spoke fluent Spanish, which he used to help Spanish-speaking immigrants in Wyoming, and was a volunteer for many worthy causes, including as a judge for a juvenile drug court, where he counseled and encouraged youngsters to reform their lives.

Al was married to a congresswoman, and when she went on Obamacare, he did too (it's a myth that members of Congress are exempted from the law). Al and his wife signed up in person at the Congressional Member Benefits (CMB) office. But then bureaucratic snafus began. They received written notices that they were *not* enrolled. But when the congresswoman's staff checked with the CMB office, they were told they *were* enrolled. This happened repeatedly.

Meanwhile, Al was experiencing chest pains. Insurance claims for his doctor visits were rejected with claims, once again, that he was *not* enrolled.

Al's doctor advised him to take a stress test, but Al became so frustrated with the Obamacare paperwork and hassles that he skipped it.

On October 24, 2014, he died in his sleep of a massive heart attack. I believe Al died a victim of Obamacare.[1] Its bureaucracy and delays, its creations of scores of new government agencies functioning outside the effective oversight of Congress, meant that Al received less good medical care than he would have done before. Al was a man who took care of himself. He exercised, he ate right—but he couldn't get around a bureaucracy that micromanages health care to all our detriments, even fatally. Al's story is not unusual. Many Americans are experiencing higher medical costs, lengthy and dangerous delays in care, and paperwork headaches from the Obamacare bureaucracy.

The Affordable Care Act, as Obamacare is officially known, filled well over 2,000 pages, and represented the single greatest expansion of Washington power since the New Deal. Not one Republican voted for it. It has now proven to be the disaster so many warned it would be.

It only narrowly passed Congress, and some Democrats had to be bullied or bribed with favors to vote for it. Then-Senate Majority Leader Harry Reid offered Democrat Ben Nelson of Nebraska $100 million in Medicaid support for his state if he would vote for the legislation. Democrat Mary Landrieu of Louisiana was promised between $200 and $300 million in Medicaid funding for her state to change her vote. Due to a drafting error, the law ended up paying out $4.3 billion instead.[2] Nelson chose not to seek reelection. Landrieu lost her next election bid to a Republican. Obamacare would not have passed without their support.

Congressional corruption is not harmless. We cannot afford to shrug our shoulders, look the other way, and hope someone else will deal with it. When congressional leaders and members put their own self-interests ahead of what is best for the American people, the American people pay a high price. When our leaders in Washington use government for their own gain, rather than serving the good of the nation, real people suffer.

WHAT YOU CAN DO

Throughout this book I have been frankly critical of my own party, because we have had congressional majority and have done very little with it. But the Democrats who have dominated Congress for decades are far worse. The Republican Party is at least pledged to the ideal of a smaller federal government. Democrats want to expand the swamp and feed the alligators.

President Obama oversaw the single greatest expansion of the federal government in my lifetime. Under his administration, our national debt exploded to unprecedented levels. His solution was more spending, more federal control, and more protection for the swamp people in Washington.

Hillary Clinton pushed for an even greater expansion of government and no one more typifies Washington than the Clintons.

Thankfully, the American people chose a different path. They elected a man, Donald J. Trump, who was explicitly opposed to Washington business as usual.

Trump's election is cause for hope, but we need to make sure that he and the Republican Congress successfully work together to make that hope real in terms of policy and reform.

Here are three things that each one of us can do to advance the cause of draining the swamp:

1. Get involved with Article V efforts in your state. The Constitution gives us this power to reform Congress and the federal government and we need to use it. It starts with getting informed about the process. Two books can help: Mark Levin's *The Liberty Amendments: Restoring the American Republic* and Tom Coburn's *Fight Back America: How We the People Can Stop Big Government with Article V* are both excellent guides to how the process works and what we can achieve. Our top priority has to be a balanced budget amendment, but we can do much more. All, however, is dependent on our active engagement as citizens. And that includes getting involved in state and local politics as well.

2. Choose public servants of character. The best-laid forms of government will fail unless upheld by men and women of character. As the essayist Montesquieu wrote, "More states have perished because of a violation of their mores [morals] than because of a violation of the Laws." Even if we ratify the best amendments and devise the wisest of rules in Congress, we will still need men and woman of virtue who can resist the temptation to put political self-interest ahead of our national well-being. What's happening in Washington today is immoral. Changing the rules will motivate Congress to do the right things, but it will take moral leaders to ensure it stays that way. As James Madison noted:

To suppose that any form of government can secure liberty or happiness without virtue in the people is a chimerical idea. If there be sufficient virtue and intelligence in the community, it will be exercised in the selection of these men. So that we do not depend on their virtue, or put confidence in our rulers, but in the people who are to choose them.[3]

The immorality we see in Congress is only an exaggerated version of the immorality we have grown too used to seeing in our culture—in businessmen who cut corners and then seek federal bailouts, in journalists and professors who act like propagandists, in homeowners who walk away from mortgages, and the list can go on. Who pays for such immorality? We all do, but our children and grandchildren most of all.

It might be hard to reform a culture. But ultimately that's what we're talking about. We need to elect men and women of character, but we also, all of us, need to be men and women of character. We need to promote character in our families, our neighborhoods, and our schools; we need to be a nation of character in every way possible.

3. Hold officeholders accountable. We can pass amendments. We can elect leaders of character and try to be better people ourselves. But unless we are vigilant in holding our elected leaders accountable we will never succeed. Liberty is always at risk. Men and women who wield power almost always seem to want more of it. It is our duty as citizens to elect the best people we can find and then keep an eye on them to make sure they enact the reforms our country needs. We, the people, are in charge. Our elected officials are supposed to work for us. We need to make sure they do a good job—or we need to fire them and hire new people. That's what elections are all about. We need to stay informed and use our voting power wisely.

IT STARTS WITH YOU

I didn't go to Congress to splash in the swamp, I went to drain it. But I and those who think like me need your help. We need you to demand change in Washington, and we need your prayers—for our efforts and our country.

Ronald Reagan warned us that, "Freedom is never more than one generation away from extinction. We didn't pass it to our children in the bloodstream. It must be fought for, protected, and handed on for them to do the same."[4]

The massive, debilitating debt Congress is handing our children and grandchildren is a form of bondage. It is immoral. It is corrupt. And it must not be permitted to continue. The time has come for brave men and women to do something.

And it starts with us.

APPENDIX A

APPLICATION FOR A
CONVENTION OF THE STATES
UNDER ARTICLE V OF
THE CONSTITUTION OF THE
UNITED STATES

Whereas, the Founders of our Constitution empowered State Legislators to be guardians of liberty against future abuses of power by the federal government, and

Whereas, the federal government has created a crushing national debt through improper and imprudent spending, and

Whereas, the federal government has invaded the legitimate roles of the states through the manipulative process of federal mandates, most of which are unfunded to a great extent, and

Whereas, the federal government has ceased to live under a proper interpretation of the Constitution of the United States, and

Whereas, it is the solemn duty of the States to protect the liberty of our people—particularly for the generations to come—by proposing Amendments to the Constitution of the United States through a

Convention of the States under Article V for the purpose of restraining these and related abuses of power,

Be it therefore resolved by the legislature of the State of _____:

Section 1. The legislature of the State of _____ hereby applies to Congress, under the provisions of Article V of the Constitution of the United States, for the calling of a convention of the states limited to proposing amendments to the Constitution of the United States that impose fiscal restraints on the federal government, limit the power and jurisdiction of the federal government, and limit the terms of office for its officials and for members of Congress.

Section 2. The secretary of state is hereby directed to transmit copies of this application to the President and Secretary of the United States Senate and to the Speaker and Clerk of the United States House of Representatives, and copies to the members of the said Senate and House of Representatives from this State; also to transmit copies hereof to the presiding officers of each of the legislative houses in the several States, requesting their cooperation.

Section 3. This application constitutes a continuing application in accordance with Article V of the Constitution of the United States until the legislatures of at least two-thirds of the several states have made applications on the same subject.

www.cosaction.com

THE CONSTITUTION OF THE UNITED STATES

PREAMBLE

We the People of the United States, in Order to form a more perfect Union, establish Justice, insure domestic Tranquility, provide for the common defense, promote the general Welfare, and secure the Blessings of Liberty to ourselves and our Posterity, do ordain and establish this Constitution for the United States of America.

ARTICLE I

SECTION 1

All legislative Powers herein granted shall be vested in a Congress of the United States, which shall consist of a Senate and House of Representatives.

SECTION 2

The House of Representatives shall be composed of Members chosen every second Year by the People of the several States, and the Electors in each State shall have the Qualifications requisite for Electors of the most numerous Branch of the State Legislature.

No Person shall be a Representative who shall not have attained to the Age of twenty five Years, and been seven Years a Citizen of the United States, and who shall not, when elected, be an Inhabitant of that State in which he shall be chosen.

Representatives and direct Taxes shall be apportioned among the several States which may be included within this Union, according to their respective Numbers, which shall be determined by adding to the whole Number of free Persons, including those bound to Service for a Term of Years, and excluding Indians not taxed, three fifths of all other Persons. The actual Enumeration shall be made within three Years after the first Meeting of the Congress of the United States, and within every subsequent Term of ten Years, in such Manner as they shall by Law direct. The Number of Representatives shall not exceed one for every thirty Thousand, but each State shall have at Least one Representative; and until such enumeration shall be made, the State of New Hampshire shall be entitled to choose three, Massachusetts eight, Rhode-Island and Providence Plantations one, Connecticut five, New-York six, New Jersey four, Pennsylvania eight, Delaware one, Maryland six, Virginia ten, North Carolina five, South Carolina five, and Georgia three.

When vacancies happen in the Representation from any State, the Executive Authority thereof shall issue Writs of Election to fill such Vacancies.

The House of Representatives shall choose their Speaker and other Officers; and shall have the sole Power of Impeachment.

SECTION 3

The Senate of the United States shall be composed of two Senators from each State, chosen by the Legislature thereof, for six Years; and each Senator shall have one Vote.

Immediately after they shall be assembled in Consequence of the first Election, they shall be divided as equally as may be into three Classes. The Seats of the Senators of the first Class shall be vacated at the Expiration of the second Year, of the second Class at the Expiration of the fourth Year, and of the third Class at the Expiration of the sixth Year, so that one third may be chosen every second Year; and if Vacancies happen by Resignation, or otherwise, during the Recess of the Legislature of any State, the Executive thereof may make temporary Appointments until the next Meeting of the Legislature, which shall then fill such Vacancies.

No Person shall be a Senator who shall not have attained to the Age of thirty Years, and been nine Years a Citizen of the United States, and who shall not, when elected, be an Inhabitant of that State for which he shall be chosen.

The Vice President of the United States shall be President of the Senate, but shall have no Vote, unless they be equally divided.

The Senate shall choose their other Officers, and also a President pro tempore, in the Absence of the Vice President, or when he shall exercise the Office of President of the United States.

The Senate shall have the sole Power to try all Impeachments. When sitting for that Purpose, they shall be on Oath or Affirmation. When the President of the United States is tried, the Chief Justice shall preside: And no Person shall be convicted without the Concurrence of two thirds of the Members present.

Judgment in Cases of Impeachment shall not extend further than to removal from Office, and disqualification to hold and enjoy any

Office of honor, Trust or Profit under the United States: but the Party convicted shall nevertheless be liable and subject to Indictment, Trial, Judgment and Punishment, according to Law.

SECTION 4

The Times, Places and Manner of holding Elections for Senators and Representatives, shall be prescribed in each State by the Legislature thereof; but the Congress may at any time by Law make or alter such Regulations, except as to the Places of choosing Senators.

The Congress shall assemble at least once in every Year, and such Meeting shall be on the first Monday in December, unless they shall by Law appoint a different Day.

SECTION 5

Each House shall be the Judge of the Elections, Returns and Qualifications of its own Members, and a Majority of each shall constitute a Quorum to do Business; but a smaller Number may adjourn from day to day, and may be authorized to compel the Attendance of absent Members, in such Manner, and under such Penalties as each House may provide.

Each House may determine the Rules of its Proceedings, punish its Members for disorderly Behaviour, and, with the Concurrence of two thirds, expel a Member.

Each House shall keep a Journal of its Proceedings, and from time to time publish the same, excepting such Parts as may in their Judgment require Secrecy; and the Yeas and Nays of the Members of either House on any question shall, at the Desire of one fifth of those Present, be entered on the Journal.

Neither House, during the Session of Congress, shall, without the Consent of the other, adjourn for more than three days, nor to any other Place than that in which the two Houses shall be sitting.

SECTION 6

The Senators and Representatives shall receive a Compensation for their Services, to be ascertained by Law, and paid out of the Treasury of the United States. They shall in all Cases, except Treason, Felony and Breach of the Peace, be privileged from Arrest during their Attendance at the Session of their respective Houses, and in going to and returning from the same; and for any Speech or Debate in either House, they shall not be questioned in any other Place.

No Senator or Representative shall, during the Time for which he was elected, be appointed to any civil Office under the Authority of the United States, which shall have been created, or the Emoluments whereof shall have been increased during such time; and no Person holding any Office under the United States, shall be a Member of either House during his Continuance in Office.

SECTION 7

All Bills for raising Revenue shall originate in the House of Representatives; but the Senate may propose or concur with Amendments as on other Bills.

Every Bill which shall have passed the House of Representatives and the Senate, shall, before it become a Law, be presented to the President of the United States: If he approve he shall sign it, but if not he shall return it, with his Objections to that House in which it shall have originated, who shall enter the Objections at large on their Journal, and proceed to reconsider it. If after such Reconsideration two thirds of that House shall agree to pass the Bill, it shall be sent, together with the Objections, to the other House, by which it shall likewise be reconsidered, and if approved by two thirds of that House, it shall become a Law. But in all such Cases the Votes of both Houses shall be determined by Yeas and Nays, and the Names of the Persons voting for and against the Bill shall be entered on the Journal of each House respectively. If any Bill shall not be returned by the President within ten Days (Sundays excepted) after it shall have been presented to him, the Same shall be a Law, in like Manner as if he had signed it, unless the Congress by their Adjournment prevent its Return, in which Case it shall not be a Law.

Every Order, Resolution, or Vote to which the Concurrence of the Senate and House of Representatives may be necessary (except on a question of Adjournment) shall be presented to the President of the United States; and before the Same shall take Effect, shall be approved by him, or being disapproved by him, shall be repassed by two thirds of the Senate and House of Representatives, according to the Rules and Limitations prescribed in the Case of a Bill.

SECTION 8

The Congress shall have Power To lay and collect Taxes, Duties, Imposts and Excises, to pay the Debts and provide for the common Defence and general Welfare of the United States; but all Duties, Imposts and Excises shall be uniform throughout the United States;

To borrow Money on the credit of the United States;

To regulate Commerce with foreign Nations, and among the several States, and with the Indian Tribes;

To establish an uniform Rule of Naturalization, and uniform Laws on the subject of Bankruptcies throughout the United States;

To coin Money, regulate the Value thereof, and of foreign Coin, and fix the Standard of Weights and Measures;

To provide for the Punishment of counterfeiting the Securities and current Coin of the United States;

To establish Post Offices and post Roads;

To promote the Progress of Science and useful Arts, by securing for limited Times to Authors and Inventors the exclusive Right to their respective Writings and Discoveries;

To constitute Tribunals inferior to the supreme Court;

To define and punish Piracies and Felonies committed on the high Seas, and Offences against the Law of Nations;

To declare War, grant Letters of Marque and Reprisal, and make Rules concerning Captures on Land and Water;

To raise and support Armies, but no Appropriation of Money to that Use shall be for a longer Term than two Years;

To provide and maintain a Navy;

To make Rules for the Government and Regulation of the land and naval Forces;

To provide for calling forth the Militia to execute the Laws of the Union, suppress Insurrections and repel Invasions;

To provide for organizing, arming, and disciplining, the Militia, and for governing such Part of them as may be employed in the Service of the United States, reserving to the States respectively, the Appointment of the Officers, and the Authority of training the Militia according to the discipline prescribed by Congress;

To exercise exclusive Legislation in all Cases whatsoever, over such District (not exceeding ten Miles square) as may, by Cession of particular States, and the Acceptance of Congress, become the Seat of the Government of the United States, and to exercise like Authority over all Places purchased by the Consent of the Legislature of the State in which the Same shall be, for the Erection of Forts, Magazines, Arsenals, dock-Yards, and other needful Buildings;-And

To make all Laws which shall be necessary and proper for carrying into Execution the foregoing Powers, and all other Powers vested by this Constitution in the Government of the United States, or in any Department or Officer thereof.

SECTION 9

The Migration or Importation of such Persons as any of the States now existing shall think proper to admit, shall not be prohibited by the Congress prior to the Year one thousand eight hundred and eight, but a Tax or duty may be imposed on such Importation, not exceeding ten dollars for each Person.

The Privilege of the Writ of Habeas Corpus shall not be suspended, unless when in Cases of Rebellion or Invasion the public Safety may require it.

No Bill of Attainder or ex post facto Law shall be passed.

No Capitation, or other direct, Tax shall be laid, unless in Proportion to the Census or enumeration herein before directed to be taken.

No Tax or Duty shall be laid on Articles exported from any State.

No Preference shall be given by any Regulation of Commerce or Revenue to the Ports of one State over those of another; nor shall Vessels bound to, or from, one State, be obliged to enter, clear, or pay Duties in another.

No Money shall be drawn from the Treasury, but in Consequence of Appropriations made by Law; and a regular Statement and Account of the Receipts and Expenditures of all public Money shall be published from time to time.

No Title of Nobility shall be granted by the United States: And no Person holding any Office of Profit or Trust under them, shall, without the Consent of the Congress, accept of any present, Emolument, Office, or Title, of any kind whatever, from any King, Prince, or foreign State.

SECTION 10

No State shall enter into any Treaty, Alliance, or Confederation; grant Letters of Marque and Reprisal; coin Money; emit Bills of Credit; make any Thing but gold and silver Coin a Tender in Payment of Debts; pass any Bill of Attainder, ex post facto Law, or Law impairing the Obligation of Contracts, or grant any Title of Nobility.

No State shall, without the Consent of the Congress, lay any Imposts or Duties on Imports or Exports, except what may be absolutely necessary for executing its inspection Laws: and the net Produce of all Duties and Imposts, laid by any State on Imports or Exports, shall be for the Use of the Treasury of the United States; and all such Laws shall be subject to the Revision and Control of the Congress.

No State shall, without the Consent of Congress, lay any Duty of Tonnage, keep Troops, or Ships of War in time of Peace, enter into any Agreement or Compact with another State, or with a foreign Power, or engage in War, unless actually invaded, or in such imminent Danger as will not admit of delay.

ARTICLE II

SECTION 1

The executive Power shall be vested in a President of the United States of America. He shall hold his Office during the Term of four Years, and, together with the Vice President, chosen for the same Term, be elected, as follows:

Each State shall appoint, in such Manner as the Legislature thereof may direct, a Number of Electors, equal to the whole Number of Senators and Representatives to which the State may be entitled in the Congress: but no Senator or Representative, or Person holding an

Office of Trust or Profit under the United States, shall be appointed an Elector.

The Electors shall meet in their respective States, and vote by Ballot for two Persons, of whom one at least shall not be an Inhabitant of the same State with themselves. And they shall make a List of all the Persons voted for, and of the Number of Votes for each; which List they shall sign and certify, and transmit sealed to the Seat of the Government of the United States, directed to the President of the Senate. The President of the Senate shall, in the Presence of the Senate and House of Representatives, open all the Certificates, and the Votes shall then be counted. The Person having the greatest Number of Votes shall be the President, if such Number be a Majority of the whole Number of Electors appointed; and if there be more than one who have such Majority, and have an equal Number of Votes, then the House of Representatives shall immediately choose by Ballot one of them for President; and if no Person have a Majority, then from the five highest on the List the said House shall in like Manner choose the President. But in choosing the President, the Votes shall be taken by States, the Representatives from each State having one Vote; a quorum for this Purpose shall consist of a Member or Members from two thirds of the States, and a Majority of all the States shall be necessary to a Choice. In every Case, after the Choice of the President, the Person having the greatest Number of Votes of the Electors shall be the Vice President. But if there should remain two or more who have equal Votes, the Senate shall choose from them by Ballot the Vice-President.

The Congress may determine the Time of choosing the Electors, and the Day on which they shall give their Votes; which Day shall be the same throughout the United States.

No Person except a natural born Citizen, or a Citizen of the United States, at the time of the Adoption of this Constitution, shall be eligible to the Office of President; neither shall any person be eligible to that Office who shall not have attained to the Age of thirty five Years, and been fourteen Years a Resident within the United States.

In Case of the Removal of the President from Office, or of his Death, Resignation, or Inability to discharge the Powers and Duties of the said Office, the Same shall devolve on the Vice President, and the Congress may by Law provide for the Case of Removal, Death, Resignation or Inability, both of the President and Vice President, declaring what Officer shall then act as President, and such Officer shall act accordingly, until the Disability be removed, or a President shall be elected.

The President shall, at stated Times, receive for his Services, a Compensation, which shall neither be increased nor diminished during the Period for which he shall have been elected, and he shall not receive within that Period any other Emolument from the United States, or any of them.

Before he enter on the Execution of his Office, he shall take the following Oath or Affirmation:-"I do solemnly swear (or affirm) that I will faithfully execute the Office of President of the United States, and will to the best of my Ability, preserve, protect and defend the Constitution of the United States."

SECTION 2

The President shall be Commander in Chief of the Army and Navy of the United States, and of the Militia of the several States, when called into the actual Service of the United States; he may require the Opinion, in writing, of the principal Officer in each of the executive Departments, upon any Subject relating to the Duties of their respective Offices, and he shall have Power to Grant Reprieves and Pardons for Offences against the United States, except in Cases of Impeachment.

He shall have Power, by and with the Advice and Consent of the Senate, to make Treaties, provided two thirds of the Senators present concur; and he shall nominate, and by and with the Advice and Consent of the Senate, shall appoint Ambassadors, other public Ministers and Consuls, Judges of the supreme Court, and all other Officers of the United States, whose Appointments are not herein otherwise provided for, and which shall be established by Law: but the Congress may by Law vest the Appointment of such inferior Officers, as they think proper, in the President alone, in the Courts of Law, or in the Heads of Departments.

The President shall have Power to fill up all Vacancies that may happen during the Recess of the Senate, by granting Commissions which shall expire at the End of their next Session.

SECTION 3

He shall from time to time give to the Congress Information on the State of the Union, and recommend to their Consideration such Measures as he shall judge necessary and expedient; he may, on extraordinary Occasions, convene both Houses, or either of them, and in Case of Disagreement between them, with Respect to the Time of Adjournment, he may adjourn them to such Time as he shall think proper; he shall receive Ambassadors and other public Ministers; he shall take Care that the Laws be faithfully executed, and shall Commission all the Officers of the United States.

SECTION 4

The President, Vice President and all Civil Officers of the United States, shall be removed from Office on Impeachment for, and Conviction of, Treason, Bribery, or other high Crimes and Misdemeanors.

ARTICLE III

SECTION 1

The judicial Power of the United States, shall be vested in one supreme Court, and in such inferior Courts as the Congress may from time to time ordain and establish. The Judges, both of the supreme and inferior Courts, shall hold their Offices during good Behaviour, and shall, at stated Times, receive for their Services, a Compensation, which shall not be diminished during their Continuance in Office.

SECTION 2

The judicial Power shall extend to all Cases, in Law and Equity, arising under this Constitution, the Laws of the United States, and Treaties made, or which shall be made, under their Authority;-to all Cases affecting Ambassadors, other public ministers and Consuls;-to all Cases of admiralty and maritime Jurisdiction;-to Controversies to which the United States shall be a Party;-to Controversies between two or more States;-between a State and Citizens of another State;-between Citizens of different States;-between Citizens of the same State claiming Lands under Grants of different States, and between a State, or the Citizens thereof, and foreign States, Citizens or Subjects.

In all Cases affecting Ambassadors, other public Ministers and Consuls, and those in which a State shall be Party, the supreme Court shall have original Jurisdiction. In all the other Cases before mentioned, the supreme Court shall have appellate Jurisdiction, both as to Law and Fact, with such Exceptions, and under such Regulations as the Congress shall make.

The Trial of all Crimes, except in Cases of Impeachment, shall be by Jury; and such Trial shall be held in the State where the said Crimes shall have been committed; but when not committed within any State, the Trial shall be at such Place or Places as the Congress may by Law have directed.

SECTION 3

Treason against the United States, shall consist only in levying War against them, or in adhering to their Enemies, giving them Aid and Comfort. No Person shall be convicted of Treason unless on the Testimony of two Witnesses to the same overt Act, or on Confession in open Court.

The Congress shall have Power to declare the Punishment of Treason, but no Attainder of Treason shall work Corruption of Blood, or Forfeiture except during the Life of the Person attainted.

ARTICLE IV

SECTION 1

Full Faith and Credit shall be given in each State to the public Acts, Records, and judicial Proceedings of every other State. And the Congress may by general Laws prescribe the Manner in which such Acts, Records and Proceedings shall be proved, and the Effect thereof.

SECTION 2

The Citizens of each State shall be entitled to all Privileges and Immunities of Citizens in the several States.

A Person charged in any State with Treason, Felony, or other Crime, who shall flee from Justice, and be found in another State, shall on Demand of the executive Authority of the State from which he fled, be delivered up, to be removed to the State having Jurisdiction of the Crime.

No Person held to Service or Labour in one State, under the Laws thereof, escaping into another, shall, in Consequence of any Law or Regulation therein, be discharged from such Service or Labour, but shall be delivered up on Claim of the Party to whom such Service or Labour may be due.

SECTION 3

New States may be admitted by the Congress into this Union; but no new State shall be formed or erected within the Jurisdiction of any other State; nor any State be formed by the Junction of two or more States, or Parts of States, without the Consent of the Legislatures of the States concerned as well as of the Congress.

The Congress shall have Power to dispose of and make all needful Rules and Regulations respecting the Territory or other Property belonging to the United States; and nothing in this Constitution shall be so construed as to Prejudice any Claims of the United States, or of any particular State.

SECTION 4

The United States shall guarantee to every State in this Union a Republican Form of Government, and shall protect each of them against Invasion; and on Application of the Legislature, or of the Executive (when the Legislature cannot be convened) against domestic Violence.

ARTICLE V

The Congress, whenever two thirds of both Houses shall deem it necessary, shall propose Amendments to this Constitution, or, on the Application of the Legislatures of two thirds of the several States, shall call a Convention for proposing Amendments, which, in either Case, shall be valid to all Intents and Purposes, as Part of this Constitution, when ratified by the Legislatures of three fourths of the several States, or by Conventions in three fourths thereof, as the one or the other Mode of Ratification may be proposed by the Congress; Provided that no Amendment which may be made prior to the Year One thousand eight hundred and eight shall in any Manner affect the first and fourth Clauses in the Ninth Section of the first Article; and that no State, without its Consent, shall be deprived of its equal Suffrage in the Senate.

ARTICLE VI

All Debts contracted and Engagements entered into, before the Adoption of this Constitution, shall be as valid against the United States under this Constitution, as under the Confederation.

This Constitution, and the Laws of the United States which shall be made in Pursuance thereof; and all Treaties made, or which shall be made, under the Authority of the United States, shall be the supreme Law of the Land; and the Judges in every State shall be bound thereby, any Thing in the Constitution or Laws of any state to the Contrary notwithstanding.

The Senators and Representatives before mentioned, and the Members of the several State Legislatures, and all executive and judicial Officers, both of the United States and of the several States, shall be bound by Oath or Affirmation, to support this Constitution; but no religious Test shall ever be required as a Qualification to any Office or public Trust under the United States.

ARTICLE VII

The Ratification of the Conventions of nine States, shall be sufficient for the Establishment of this Constitution between the States so ratifying the Same.

DONE in Convention by the Unanimous Consent of the States present the Seventeenth Day of September in the Year of our Lord one thousand seven hundred and Eighty seven and of the Independence of the United States of America the Twelfth. In WITNESS whereof We have hereunto subscribed our Names,

Go. Washington—*Presidt and deputy from Virginia*

New Hampshire: John Langdon, Nicholas Gilman.

Massachusetts: Nathaniel Gorham, Rufus King.

Connecticut: Wm. Saml. Johnson, Roger Sherman.

New York: Alexander Hamilton.

New Jersey: Wil: Livingston, David Brearley, Wm. Paterson, Jona. Dayton.

Pennsylvania: B. Franklin, Robt. Morris, Tho: Fitzsimons, James Wilson, Thomas Mifflin, Geo. Clymer, Jared Ingersoll, Gouv: Morris.

Delaware: Geo: Read, John Dickinson, Jaco: Broom, Gunning Bedford, Jun'r, Richard Bassett.

Maryland: James M'Henry, Danl Carroll, Dan: of St. Thos. Jenifer.

Virginia: John Blair, James Madison, Jr.

North Carolina: Wm. Blount, Hu. Williamson, Rich'd Dobbs Spaight.

South Carolina: J. Rutledge, Charles Pinckney, Charles Cotesworth Pinckney, Pierce Butler.

Georgia William: Few, Abr. Baldwin

Attest: William Jackson, Secretary

AMENDMENT I

Congress shall make no law respecting an establishment of religion, or prohibiting the free exercise thereof; or abridging the freedom of speech, or of the press; or the right of the people peaceably to assemble, and to petition the Government for a redress of grievances.

AMENDMENT II

A well regulated Militia, being necessary to the security of a free State, the right of the people to keep and bear Arms, shall not be infringed.

AMENDMENT III

No Soldier shall, in time of peace be quartered in any house, without the consent of the Owner, nor in time of war, but in a manner to be prescribed by law.

AMENDMENT IV

The right of the people to be secure in their persons, houses, papers, and effects, against unreasonable searches and seizures, shall not be violated, and no Warrants shall issue, but upon probable cause, supported by Oath or affirmation, and particularly describing the place to be searched, and the persons or things to be seized.

AMENDMENT V

No person shall be held to answer for a capital, or otherwise infamous crime, unless on a presentment or indictment of a Grand

Jury, except in cases arising in the land or naval forces, or in the Militia, when in actual service in time of War or public danger; nor shall any person be subject for the same offence to be twice put in jeopardy of life or limb; nor shall be compelled in any criminal case to be a witness against himself, nor be deprived of life, liberty, or property, without due process of law; nor shall private property be taken for public use, without just compensation.

AMENDMENT VI

In all criminal prosecutions, the accused shall enjoy the right to a speedy and public trial, by an impartial jury of the State and district wherein the crime shall have been committed, which district shall have been previously ascertained by law, and to be informed of the nature and cause of the accusation; to be confronted with the witnesses against him; to have compulsory process for obtaining witnesses in his favor, and to have the Assistance of Counsel for his defence.

AMENDMENT VII

In Suits at common law, where the value in controversy shall exceed twenty dollars, the right of trial by jury shall be preserved, and no fact tried by a jury, shall be otherwise re-examined in any Court of the United States, than according to the rules of the common law.

AMENDMENT VIII

Excessive bail shall not be required, nor excessive fines imposed, nor cruel and unusual punishments inflicted.

AMENDMENT IX

The enumeration in the Constitution, of certain rights, shall not be construed to deny or disparage others retained by the people.

AMENDMENT X

The powers not delegated to the United States by the Constitution, nor prohibited by it to the States, are reserved to the States respectively, or to the people.

AMENDMENT XI

The Judicial power of the United States shall not be construed to extend to any suit in law or equity, commenced or prosecuted against one of the United States by Citizens of another State, or by Citizens or Subjects of any Foreign State.

AMENDMENT XII

The Electors shall meet in their respective states and vote by ballot for President and Vice-President, one of whom, at least, shall not be an inhabitant of the same state with themselves; they shall name in their ballots the person voted for as President, and in distinct ballots the person voted for as Vice-President, and they shall make distinct lists of all persons voted for as President, and of all persons voted for as Vice-President, and of the number of votes for each, which lists they shall sign and certify, and transmit sealed to the seat of the government of the United States, directed to the President of the Senate;-The President of the Senate shall, in the presence of the Senate and House of Representatives, open all the certificates and the votes shall then be counted;-

The person having the greatest Number of votes for President, shall be the President, if such number be a majority of the whole number of Electors appointed; and if no person have such majority, then from the persons having the highest numbers not exceeding three on the list of those voted for as President, the House of Representatives shall choose immediately, by ballot, the President. But in choosing the President, the votes shall be taken by states, the representation from each state having one vote; a quorum for this purpose shall consist of a member or members from two-thirds of the states, and a majority of all the states shall be necessary to a choice. And if the House of Representatives shall not choose a President whenever the right of choice shall devolve upon them, before the fourth day of March next following, then the Vice-President shall act as President, as in the case of the death or other constitutional disability of the President-The person having the greatest number of votes as Vice-President, shall be the Vice-President, if such number be a majority of the whole number of Electors appointed, and if no person have a majority, then from the two highest numbers on the list, the Senate shall choose the Vice-President; a quorum for the purpose shall consist of two-thirds of the whole number of Senators, and a majority of the whole number shall be necessary to a choice. But no person constitutionally ineligible to the office of President shall be eligible to that of Vice-President of the United States.

AMENDMENT XIII

SECTION 1

Neither slavery nor involuntary servitude, except as a punishment for crime whereof the party shall have been duly convicted, shall exist within the United States, or any place subject to their jurisdiction.

SECTION 2

Congress shall have power to enforce this article by appropriate legislation.

AMENDMENT XIV

SECTION 1

All persons born or naturalized in the United States and subject to the jurisdiction thereof, are citizens of the United States and of the State wherein they reside. No State shall make or enforce any law which shall abridge the privileges or immunities of citizens of the United States; nor shall any State deprive any person of life, liberty, or property, without due process of law; nor deny to any person within its jurisdiction the equal protection of the laws.

SECTION 2

Representatives shall be apportioned among the several States according to their respective numbers, counting the whole number of persons in each State, excluding Indians not taxed. But when the right to vote at any election for the choice of electors for President and Vice President of the United States, Representatives in Congress, the Executive and Judicial officers of a State, or the members of the Legislature thereof, is denied to any of the male inhabitants of such State, being twenty-one years of age, and citizens of the United States, or in any way abridged, except for participation in rebellion, or other crime, the basis of representation therein shall be reduced in the proportion which the number of such male citizens shall bear to the whole number of male citizens twenty-one years of age in such State.

SECTION 3

No person shall be a Senator or Representative in Congress, or elector of President and Vice President, or hold any office, civil or military, under the United States, or under any State, who, having previously taken an oath, as a member of Congress, or as an officer of the United States, or as a member of any State legislature, or as an executive or judicial officer of any State, to support the Constitution of the United States, shall have engaged in insurrection or rebellion against the same, or given aid or comfort to the enemies thereof. But Congress may by a vote of two-thirds of each House, remove such disability.

SECTION 4

The validity of the public debt of the United States, authorized by law, including debts incurred for payment of pensions and bounties for services in suppressing insurrection or rebellion, shall not be questioned. But neither the United States nor any State shall assume or pay any debt or obligation incurred in aid of insurrection or rebellion against the United States, or any claim for the loss or emancipation of any slave; but all such debts, obligations and claims shall be held illegal and void.

SECTION 5

The Congress shall have power to enforce, by appropriate legislation, the provisions of this article.

AMENDMENT XV

SECTION 1

The right of citizens of the United States to vote shall not be denied or abridged by the United States or by any State on account of race, color, or previous condition of servitude.

SECTION 2

The Congress shall have power to enforce this article by appropriate legislation.

AMENDMENT XVI

The Congress shall have power to lay and collect taxes on incomes, from whatever source derived, without apportionment among the several States, and without regard to any census or enumeration.

AMENDMENT XVII

The Senate of the United States shall be composed of two Senators from each State, elected by the people thereof, for six years; and each Senator shall have one vote. The electors in each State shall have the qualifications requisite for electors of the most numerous branch of the State legislatures.

When vacancies happen in the representation of any State in the Senate, the executive authority of such State shall issue writs of election to fill such vacancies: Provided, That the legislature of any State may empower the executive thereof to make temporary appointments until the people fill the vacancies by election as the legislature may direct.

This amendment shall not be so construed as to affect the election or term of any Senator chosen before it becomes valid as part of the Constitution.

AMENDMENT XVIII

SECTION 1

After one year from the ratification of this article the manufacture, sale, or transportation of intoxicating liquors within, the importation thereof into, or the exportation thereof from the United States and all territory subject to the jurisdiction thereof for beverage purposes is hereby prohibited.

SECTION 2

The Congress and the several States shall have concurrent power to enforce this article by appropriate legislation.

SECTION 3

This article shall be inoperative unless it shall have been ratified as an amendment to the Constitution by the legislatures of the several States, as provided in the Constitution, within seven years from the date of the submission hereof to the States by the Congress.

AMENDMENT XIX

The right of citizens of the United States to vote shall not be denied or abridged by the United States or by any State on account of sex.

Congress shall have power to enforce this article by appropriate legislation.

AMENDMENT XX

SECTION 1

The terms of the President and Vice President shall end at noon on the 20th day of January, and the terms of Senators and Representatives at noon on the third day of January, of the years in which such terms would have ended if this article had not been ratified; and the terms of their successors shall then begin.

SECTION 2

The Congress shall assemble at least once in every year, and such meeting shall begin at noon on the 3d day of January, unless they shall by law appoint a different day.

SECTION 3

If, at the time fixed for the beginning of the term of the President, the President elect shall have died, the Vice President elect shall become President. If a President shall not have been chosen before the time fixed for the beginning of his term, or if the President elect shall have failed to qualify, then the Vice President elect shall act as President until a President shall have qualified; and the Congress may by law provide for the case wherein neither a President elect nor a Vice President elect shall have qualified, declaring who shall then act as President, or the manner in which one who is to act shall be selected, and such person shall act accordingly until a President or Vice President shall have qualified.

SECTION 4

The Congress may by law provide for the case of the death of any of the persons from whom the House of Representatives may choose a President whenever the right of choice shall have devolved upon them, and for the case of the death of any of the persons from whom the Senate may choose a Vice President whenever the right of choice shall have devolved upon them.

SECTION 5

Sections 1 and 2 shall take effect on the 15th day of October following the ratification of this article.

SECTION 6

This article shall be inoperative unless it shall have been ratified as an amendment to the Constitution by the legislatures of three-fourths of the several States within seven years from the date of its submission.

AMENDMENT XXI

SECTION 1

The eighteenth article of amendment to the Constitution of the United States is hereby repealed.

SECTION 2

The transportation or importation into any State, Territory, or possession of the United States for delivery or use therein of intoxicating liquors, in violation of the laws thereof, is hereby prohibited.

SECTION 3

This article shall be inoperative unless it shall have been ratified as an amendment to the Constitution by conventions in the several States, as provided in the Constitution, within seven years from the date of the submission hereof to the States by the Congress.

AMENDMENT XXII

SECTION 1

No person shall be elected to the office of the President more than twice, and no person who has held the office of President, or acted as President, for more than two years of a term to which some other person was elected President shall be elected to the office of the President more than once. But this Article shall not apply to any person holding the office of President, when this Article was proposed by the Congress, and shall not prevent any person who may be holding the office of President, or acting as President, during the term within which this Article becomes operative from holding the office of President or acting as President during the remainder of such term.

SECTION 2

This article shall be inoperative unless it shall have been ratified as an amendment to the Constitution by the legislatures of three-fourths of the several States within seven years from the date of its submission to the States by the Congress.

AMENDMENT XXIII

SECTION 1

The District constituting the seat of Government of the United States shall appoint in such manner as the Congress may direct:

A number of electors of President and Vice President equal to the whole number of Senators and Representatives in Congress to which the District would be entitled if it were a State, but in no event more than the least populous State; they shall be in addition to those appointed by the States, but they shall be considered, for the purposes of the election of President and Vice President, to be electors appointed by a State; and they shall meet in the District and perform such duties as provided by the twelfth article of amendment.

SECTION 2

The Congress shall have power to enforce this article by appropriate legislation.

AMENDMENT XXIV

SECTION 1

The right of citizens of the United States to vote in any primary or other election for President or Vice President for electors for President or Vice President, or for Senator or Representative in Congress, shall not be denied or abridged by the United States or any State by reason of failure to pay any poll tax or other tax.

SECTION 2

The Congress shall have power to enforce this article by appropriate legislation.

AMENDMENT XXV

SECTION 1

In case of the removal of the President from office or of his death or resignation, the Vice President shall become President.

SECTION 2

Whenever there is a vacancy in the office of the Vice President, the President shall nominate a Vice President who shall take office upon confirmation by a majority vote of both Houses of Congress.

SECTION 3

Whenever the President transmits to the President pro tempore of the Senate and the Speaker of the House of Representatives his written declaration that he is unable to discharge the powers and duties of his office, and until he transmits to them a written declaration to the contrary, such powers and duties shall be discharged by the Vice President as Acting President.

SECTION 4

Whenever the Vice President and a majority of either the principal officers of the executive departments or of such other body as Congress may by law provide, transmit to the President pro tempore of the Senate and the Speaker of the House of Representatives their written declaration that the President is unable to discharge the powers and duties of his office, the Vice President shall immediately assume the powers and duties of the office as Acting President.

Thereafter, when the President transmits to the President pro tempore of the Senate and the Speaker of the House of Representatives his written declaration that no inability exists, he shall resume the powers and duties of his office unless the Vice President and a majority of either the principal officers of the executive department or of such other body as Congress may by law provide, transmit within four days to the President pro tempore of the Senate and the Speaker of the House of Representatives their written declaration that the

President is unable to discharge the powers and duties of his office. Thereupon Congress shall decide the issue, assembling within forty-eight hours for that purpose if not in session. If the Congress, within twenty-one days after receipt of the latter written declaration, or, if Congress is not in session, within twenty-one days after Congress is required to assemble, determines by two-thirds vote of both Houses that the President is unable to discharge the powers and duties of his office, the Vice President shall continue to discharge the same as Acting President; otherwise, the President shall resume the powers and duties of his office.

AMENDMENT XXVI

SECTION 1
The right of citizens of the United States, who are eighteen years of age or older, to vote shall not be denied or abridged by the United States or by any State on account of age.

SECTION 2
The Congress shall have power to enforce this article by appropriate legislation.

AMENDMENT XXVII

No law varying the compensation for the services of the Senators and Representatives shall take effect, until an election of Representatives shall have intervened.

NOTES

CHAPTER 1: WHY WASHINGTON IS A SWAMP

1. Brent Budowsky, "Sanders-Warren Before New Hampshire Would Rock the Nation," Observer.com, January 8, 2016, http://observer.com/2016/01/sanders-warren-before-new-hampshire-would-rock-the-nation/.
2. Geoff Colvin,"Adm. Mike Mullen: Debt is still biggest threat to U.S. security," Fortune.com, May 12, 2012, http://fortune.com/2012/05/10/adm-mike-mullen-debt-is-still-biggest-threat-to-u-s-security/.
3. Tim Mak, "Former top military officer sees national debt as biggest threat to country." *Washington Examiner*, January 21, 2014, http://www.washingtonexaminer.com/former-top-military-officer-sees-national-debt-as-biggest-threat-to-country/article/2542594.

4. "Editorial: Brat targets unfunded liabilities," *Richmond Times- Dispatch*, August 11, 2015, http://www.richmond. com/opinion/our-opinion/article_e63d45f7-d325-5d6d-a09c-60f1728fb8be.html.

5. "Freshman Class of the 112th Congress: Introduction," RealClearPolitics, March 17, 2014, http://www. realclearpolitics.com/lists/freshmen_of_the_112th_congress/.

CHAPTER 2: WELCOME TO WASHINGTON, CONGRESSMAN!

1. "Cannon Caucus Room," History, Art, & Archives: United States House of Representatives, History.house.gov, http:// history.house.gov/Exhibitions-and-Publications/Cannon-Building/Caucus-Room/.

2. "Ken Buck dishes out a slice of disrespect for the president," *Denver Post*, November 21, 2014, http://www.denverpost. com/2014/11/21/ken-buck-dishes-out-a-slice-of-disrespect-for-the-president/.

CHAPTER 3: PLAY THE GAME—OR ELSE

1. Emily Cahn, "Democrats Likely to Gain One House Seat in Florida Redraw," *Roll Call,* August 5, 2015, http://www. rollcall.com/news/democrats-likely-gain-one-house-seat-florida-redraw.

2. Caroline May, "Rep. Steve King Travels to Egypt in Defiance of GOP Leadership," Breitbart, March 16, 2015, http://www. breitbart.com/big-government/2015/03/16/rep-steve-king-travels-to-egypt-in-defiance-of-gop-leadership/.

3. Meadows, Mark. Personal interview. September 6, 2016.

4. Cynthia Lummis, personal interview, September 1, 2016.

5. Emily Cahn, "Exclusive: NRCC Announces 12 Members in Patriot Program," *Roll Call*, February 13, 2015, http://www.rollcall.com/politics/nrcc-patriot-program-2016/.

6. Lee Drutman, "Ways and Means, Financial Services, and Energy and Commerce are top House fundraising committees," Sunlight Foundation, April 2, 2012, http://sunlightfoundation.com/2012/04/02/housecommittees/.

7. "House Financial Services Committee," OpenSecrets.org: Center for Responsive Politics, 2016 cycle, https://www.opensecrets.org/cmteprofiles/overview.php?cmteid=H05&cmte=HFIN&congno=114&chamber=H.

8. Eric Lipton and Kevin Sack, "Fiscal Footnote: Big Senate Gift to Drug Maker," *New York Times*, January 19, 2013, http://www.nytimes.com/2013/01/20/us/medicare-pricing-delay-is-political-win-for-amgen-drug-maker.html?_r=0.

CHAPTER 4: CRISIS OF CHARACTER

1. John Adams to Mercy Otis Warren, April 16, 1776. A. Koch and W. Peden, eds., *The Selected Writings of John and John Quincy Adams* (New York: Knopf, 1946), 57.

2. Jonathan Strong, "Boehner Super-PAC Aides Push Senate Immigration Bill," National Review, August 21, 2013, http://www.nationalreview.com/corner/356401/boehner-super-pac-aides-push-senate-immigration-bill-jonathan-strong.

3. Scott Wong, "Conservatives seethe after attacks from allies of Boehner," *The Hill*, March 21, 2015, http://thehill.com/homenews/house/236503-conservatives-seethe-after-attacks-from-boehner-allies.

4. Associated Press, "Rep. Corrine Brown indicted in fraud case over charity 'slush fund,'" Fox News, July 8, 2016, http://

www.foxnews.com/politics/2016/07/08/us-rep-corrine-brown-indicted-after-fraud-investigation.html.

5. Kevin Johnson, "Former Illinois congressman Aaron Schock indicted," *USA Today*, November 10, 2016, http://www.usatoday.com/story/news/politics/2016/11/10/aaron-schock-indicted-illinois/93609124/.

6. Ledyard King, "Rep. Trey Radel resigns after drug plea," *USA Today*, January 28, 2014, http://www.usatoday.com/story/news/politics/2014/01/27/trey-radel-resign-congress-cocaine/4934741/.

7. Jordy Yager, "Ethics Committee finds Rep. Laura Richardson guilty on seven accounts," *The Hill*, August 1, 2012, http://thehill.com/homenews/house/241573-ethics-panel-finds-rep-laura-richardson-guilty-on-seven-counts.

8. Associated Press,"Former Rep. Jesse Jackson Jr. sentenced to 30 months in prison," Fox News, August 14, 2013, http://www.foxnews.com/politics/2013/08/14/former-rep-jesse-jackson-jr-to-be-sentenced.html.

9. Dennis Wagner, "Ex-U.S. Rep. Rick Renzi gets 3-year prison term," azcentral.com, October 28, 2013, http://archive.azcentral.com/news/politics/articles/20131028ex-us-rep-rick-renzi-sentenced-tucson.html.

10. Chad Pergram, "Indiana Rep. Mark Sounder Resigns After Affair with Staffer," Fox News, May 18, 2010, http://www.foxnews.com/politics/2010/05/18/exclusive-indiana-rep-mark-souder-resign-amid-affair-staffer.html.

11. Matthew Jaffe and John R. Parkinson,"Congressman Chris Lee Resigns After Shirtless Photo Posted on Internet," ABC News, February 9, 2011, http://abcnews.go.com/Politics/

congressman-chris-lee-resigns-shirtless-photo-posted-internet/
story?id=12878937.

12. Tarini Parti, "McAllister will run for full term," *Politico*, June
30, 2014, http://www.politico.com/story/2014/06/vance-
mcallister-running-full-term-louisiana-108434.

13. John Adams, October 11, 1798, letter to the officers of the
First Brigade of the Third Division of the Militia of
Massachusetts. Charles Francis Adams, ed., *The Works of
John Adams, Second President of the United States* (Boston:
Little, Brown, and Co., 1854), 9:229.

14. "Will Rogers on Politics," Willrogerstoday.com, http://www.
willrogerstoday.com/will_rogers_quotes/quotes.cfm?qID=4
(accessed November 23, 2016).

CHAPTER 5: BEATING THE BELTWAY BULLIES

1. Doug Palmer, "White House wants trade promotion
authority: Kirk," Reuters, February 29, 2012, http://www.
reuters.com/article/us-usa-trade-kirk-
idUSTRE81S1FF20120229.

2. Patrick Goddenough, "Kerry: Iran Deal Not a Treaty 'Because
You Can't Pass a Treaty Anymore,'" July 29, 2015, http://
www.cnsnews.com/news/article/patrick-goodenough/kerry-
iran-deal-not-treaty-because-you-cant-pass-treaty-anymore.

3. Emma Dumain, "Trade Rule Passes Despite Conservative
Mutiny," *Roll Call*, June 11, 2015, http://www.rollcall.com/
news/home/trade-promotion-authority-rule-conservative-
mutiny.

4. Personal interview of Mark Meadows by Bill Blankschaen.
Atlanta, Georgia, September 6, 2016.

5. "Chaffetz, Meadows Statement on Subcommittee Chairmanship," Oversight & Government Reform, June 2015, https://oversight.house.gov/release/chaffetz-meadows-statements-on-subcommittee-chairmanship/.

6. Cristina Marcos, "House freshman class president on verge of being ousted," The Hill, June 24, 2015, http://thehill.com/homenews/house/245989-conservative-freshman-class-president-on-verge-of-being-ousted.

CHAPTER 6: CORPORATE WELFARE

1. "Obama calls the Export-Import Bank 'Little more than a fund for corporate welfare.'" YouTube video, posted by club4growth, March 28, 2012, https://www.youtube.com/watch?v=0fd-4Xl9w2c.

2. Paul Merrion, "Boeing led parade of donors for Obama inaugural," *Crain's Chicago Business*, April 23, 2013, http://www.chicagobusiness.com/article/20130423/NEWS02/130429970/boeing-led-parade-of-donors-for-obama-inaugural.

3. Dan Holler, "Export-Import Bank Head: Boeing can Arrange own Financing," Heritage Action, March 12, 2014, http://heritageaction.com/2014/03/export-import-bank-head-boeing-can-arrange-financing/.

4. Timothy P. Carney, "Here's the corporate welfare agency Hillary wants to put 'on steroids,'" *Washington Examiner*, January 19, 2016, http://www.washingtonexaminer.com/heres-the-corporate-welfare-agency-hillary-wants-to-put-on-steroids/article/2580902.

5. "Ex-Im Assistance to Minority Firms, 2007," produced by Veronique de Rugy, Mercatus Center at George Mason

University, September 30, 2014, https://www.mercatus.org/
system/files/C1.-Minority-POSTER.pdf.

6. "Annual Report 2013: Export-Import Bank of the United
States," Export-Import Bank of the United States, http://www.
exim.gov/sites/default/files/reports/annual/annual-report-2013.
pdf..

7. Katherine Rosario, "Export-Import Bank: Who Really
Benefits?" Heritage Action, April 22, 2014, http://
heritageaction.com/2014/04/export-import-bank-really-
benefits/.

8. "About Us," Export-Import Bank of the United States http://
www.exim.gov/about.

9. Holler, "Export-Import Bank Head: Boeing can Arrange own
Financing."

10. Doug Cameron, "Boeing Cites Jitters Over Airplane Financing
From Ex-Im Bank," *Wall Street Journal*, August 7, 2013,
http://www.wsj.com/news/articles/SB10001424127887323477
604578654180186390150.

11. Diane Katz, "Katz: A case for ending corporate welfare," *The
Washington Times*, April 21, 2014, http://www.
washingtontimes.com/news/2014/apr/21/katz-a-case-for-
ending-corporate-welfare/.

12. Jeanne Sahadi, "U.S. deficit falls to $680 billion," CNN,
October 30, 2013, http://money.cnn.com/2013/10/30/news/
economy/deficit-2013-treasury/.

13. Timothy P. Carney, "Here's the corporate welfare agency
Hillary wants to put 'on steroids,'" *Washington Examiner*,
January 19, 2016, http://www.washingtonexaminer.com/
heres-the-corporate-welfare-agency-hillary-wants-to-put-on-
steroids/article/2580902.

14. Vicki Needham, "House panel approves bills to stop Boeing's sale of planes to Iran," *The Hill*, July 13, 2016, http://thehill. com/policy/finance/287657-house-panel-aims-to-stop-boeings-sale-of-planes-to-iran.

15. Timothy P. Carney, "Dems go to mat for mega export subsidies," Washington Examiner, June 9, 2016, http://www. washingtonexaminer.com/dems-go-to-mat-for-mega-export-subsidies/article/2593430.

16. Jim Jordan, "The Ex-Im Bank Is a Waste of Money," *National Review*, May 15, 2015, http://www.nationalreview.com/ article/418412/ex-im-bank-waste-money-jim-jordan.

17. Peter Fricke, "Export-Import Bank Accused of Conflicts of Interest," *Daily Caller*, August 1, 2014, http://dailycaller. com/2014/08/01/export-import-bank-accused-of-conflicts-of-interest/.

18. "Nominations Open for 2017 Advisory Committee," Export Import Bank of the United States, http://www.exim.gov/ about/leadership/advisory-committee.

19. Chinedu Ekweozoh, "The United States Export-Import Bank Challenges In Adapting To The Dynamic Financial Needs Of The 21st Century Business World," May 7, 2016, https:// www.linkedin.com/pulse/united-states-export-import-bank-challenges-adapting-ekweozoh-mba.

20. Nick Timiraos, "House Votes to Reauthorize U.S. Export-Import Bank," *Wall Street Journal*, http://www.wsj.com/ articles/house-votes-to-reauthorize-u-s-export-import-bank-1445986019.

21. Melissa Quinn, "62 House Republicans Join Democrats to Clear Path for Vote Reviving Export-Import Bank," *Daily Signal*, October 26, 2015, http://dailysignal.

com/2015/10/26/62-house-republicans-join-democrats-to-clear-path-for-vote-reviving-export-import-bank/.

22. Jackie Calmes, "House Votes Overwhelmingly to Reopen the Ex-Im Bank," *New York Times*, October 28, 2015, http://www.nytimes.com/2015/10/28/us/politics/house-votes-overwhelmingly-to-reopen-the-ex-im-bank.html?_r=0.

23. Mark Meadows, personal interview by Bill Blankschaen. Atlanta, Georgia, September 6, 2016.

CHAPTER 7: SWAMP-BASED ACCOUNTING

1. Matt Phillips, "The Long Story of U.S. Debt, From 1790 to 2011, in 1 Little Chart," *The Atlantic*, November 13, 2012, http://www.theatlantic.com/business/archive/2012/11/the-long-story-of-us-debt-from-1790-to-2011-in-1-little-chart/265185/.

2. "Databases, Tables & Calculators by Subject: CPI Inflation Calculator," United States Department of Labor: Bureau of Labor Statistics, http://www.bls.gov/data/inflation_calculator.htm.

3. "National Debt," Just Facts: A Resource for Independent Thinkers, http://www.justfacts.com/nationaldebt.asp.

4. "Analytical Perspectives: Budget of the U.S. Government, Fiscal Year 2016," White House Office of Management and Budget, https://www.whitehouse.gov/sites/default/files/omb/budget/fy2016/assets/spec.pdf.

5. John Cheves, "Prince of Pork: Hal Rogers Hauls Home Tax Dollars By The Billions," *Lexington Herald-Leader*, February 6, 2005.

6. "Conservatives Peeved After GOP Taps 'Prince of Pork' to Lead Spending Committee," Fox News: Politics. http://www.

foxnews.com/politics/2010/12/10/gop-taps-prince-pork-lead-committee-overseeing-federal-spending.html.

7. Ryan Alexander, "The Congress That Couldn't Shoot Straight," *US News*, http://www.usnews.com/opinion/blogs/economic-intelligence/2013/07/02/get-ready-for-more-congressional-budget-ineptitude.

8. Cynthia Lummis, phone interview by Bill Blankschaen. Atlanta, Georgia, September 1, 2016.

9. Tom Feran, "John, Boehner says Senate Dems haven't passed a budget in more than 1,000 days," PolitiFact, April 26, 2012, http://www.politifact.com/ohio/statements/2012/apr/26/john-boehner/john-boehner-says-senate-dems-havent-passed-budget/.

10. Tom Howell Jr., "Congress passes first budget in 6 years," *Washington Times*, May 5, 2015, http://www.washingtontimes.com/news/2015/may/5/senate-clears-way-final-passage-congress-budget/.

11. Angelo M. Codevilla, "After the Republic," *Claremont Review of Books*, September 27, 2016, http://www.claremont.org/crb/basicpage/after-the-republic/.

12. James Wallner, and Paul Winfree, "The Implications of Regular Lame-Duck Sessions in Congress for Representative Government," The Heritage Foundation, Backgrounder #3154 on Political Thought, September 6, 2016, http://www.heritage.org/research/reports/2016/09/the-implications-of-regular-lame-duck-sessions-in-congress-for-representative-government.

13. Jim DeMint, "Lame Ducks and Zombies: How Congress Avoids Accountability," *Daily Signal*, September 7, 2016,

http://dailysignal.com/2016/09/07/lame-ducks-and-zombies-how-congress-avoids-accountability/.

14. "The Budget and Economic Outlook: Fiscal Years 2004–2013," Congressional Budget Office, https://www.cbo.gov/sites/default/files/108th-congress-2003-2004/reports/entirereport_witherrata.pdf.

15. Ibid.

16. Mindy R. Levit et al., *Mandatory Spending Since 1962*, Congressional Research Service, March 18, 2015, https://fas.org/sgp/crs/misc/RL33074.pdf.

17. Judy Stone, "21st Century Cures Act: Pork or Promise?" *Forbes*, September 22, 2016, http://www.forbes.com/sites/judystone/2016/09/22/21st-century-cures-act-pork-or-promise/#3beb75d56818.

18. Ibid.

19. Javier Blas, "U.S. Plans to Sell Down Strategic Oil Reserve to Raise Cash," *Bloomberg*, October 27, 2015, http://www.bloomberg.com/news/articles/2015-10-27/u-s-plans-to-sell-down-strategic-oil-reserve-to-raise-cash.

20. Larry Goldstein and Lucian Pugliaresi, "Congress' bizarre idea to pay for health care," *Politico*, July 1, 2015, http://www.politico.com/agenda/story/2015/06/congress-strategic-petroleum-reserve-000125#ixzz4OsOuxBQe.

21. Keith Laing, "$305B highway bill taps Fed, oil reserves," *The Hill*, December 1, 2015, http://thehill.com/policy/transportation/261693-highway-bill-agreement-taps-fed-oil-reserves-custom-fees.

22. Romina Boccia, "Why Some Sequestration Savings Never Happened," *Daily Signal*, May 9, 2016, http://dailysignal.

com/2016/05/09/why-some-sequestration-savings-never-happened/.

CHAPTER 8: ZOMBIE GOVERNMENT

1. Craig Welch, "A brief history of the spotted-owl controversy," *The Seattle Times*, August 6, 2000, http://community. seattletimes.nwsource.com/archive/?date=20000806&s lug=4035697.

2. "Brief History of the Endangered Species Act," Coosa-Alabama River Improvement Association, http://www.caria. org/brief-history-of-the-endangered-species-actlegislative-history-of-the-endangered-species-act/.

3. Martin Matishak, "Why Is the Government Spending $310 Billion on 'Unauthorized' Programs?" *The Fiscal Times*, July 18, 2016, http://www.thefiscaltimes.com/2016/01/18/Why-Government-Spending-310-Billion-Unauthorized-Programs.

4. Danny Vinik, "Meet your unauthorized federal government," *Politico*, February 3, 2016, http://www.politico.com/agenda/story/2016/02/government-agencies-programs-unauthorized-000036-000037.

5. See Rule XXI of the House Rules and Manual, H. Doc. 110–162, pp. 836–891.

6. Louis Jacobson, "Only 1 percent of endangered species list has been taken off list, says Cynthia Lummis," PolitiFact, September 3, 2013, http://www.politifact.com/truth-o-meter/statements/2013/sep/03/cynthia-lummis/endangered-species-act-percent-taken-off-list/.

7. Jeff Flake, *Wastebook: The Farce Awakens*, December 2015, http://www.flake.senate.gov/public/_cache/files/03714fa3-

e01d-46a1-9c19-299533056741/final-wastebook-2015-pdf.
pdf.

8. Terence P. Jeffrey, "Federal Debt in FY 2016 Jumped
    $1,422,827,047,452.46—That's $12,036 Per Household,"
    CNS News, October 3, 2016, http://www.cnsnews.com/news/
    article/terence-p-jeffrey/federal-debt-fy-2016-
    jumped-142282704745246.

9. "Meth Lab Explosion Exposes Culture of Misconduct at
    NIST Facility," Committee on Science, Space, & Technology,
    Press Release, September 30, 2015, https://science.house.gov/
    news/press-releases/meth-lab-explosion-exposes-culture-
    misconduct-nist-facility.

10. Andrew Blake, "Meth experiment gone bad blamed for
    explosion at NIST lab; ex-guard to plead guilty," *Washington
    Times*, August 19, 2015, http://www.washingtontimes.com/
    news/2015/aug/19/meth-experiment-gone-bad-blamed-
    explosion-nist-lab/.

11. "FY 2016 Fall Grant Announcement," National Endowment
    for the Arts, December 8, 2015, https://www.arts.gov/sites/
    default/files/Fall_2015_State_grant_list.pdf.

12. Lindsey Burke and David B. Muhlhausen Ph.D., "Head Start
    Impact Evaluation Report Finally Released," The Heritage
    Foundation, Issue Brief #3823, January 10, 2013, http://www.
    heritage.org/research/reports/2013/01/head-start-impact-
    evaluation-report-finally-released.

13. Michael Bastasch and Ethan Barton, "Feds Hand Over Nearly
    $50 MILLION In Environmental Lawsuits," *Daily Caller*,
    August 9, 2016, http://dailycaller.com/2016/08/09/feds-hand-
    over-nearly-50-million-in-environmental-lawsuits/.

14. Examiner Editorial, "EPA's back-room 'sue and settle' deals require reform," *Washington Examiner,* May 25, 2013, http://www.washingtonexaminer.com/epas-back-room-sue-and-settle-deals-require-reform/article/2530505.

15. Bastasch and Barton, "Feds Hand Over Nearly $50 MILLION In Environmental Lawsuits."

16. "Lawsuit challenges feds over 'sue and settle' tactics on endangered species," Fox News: Politics, March 18, 2014, http://www.foxnews.com/politics/2014/03/18/lawsuit-challenges-feds-over-sue-and-settle-tactics-on-endangered-species.html.

17. "Weekly Newsletter- 8/26/16," Endangered Species Watch, August 8, 26, 2016, http://esawatch.org/weekly-newsletter-82616/.

18. Examiner Editorial, "EPA's back-room 'sue and settle' deals require reform."

19. Doc Hastings and Cynthia Lummis, "Improving the Endangered Species Act for the 21st century," Daily Caller, March 11, 2014, http://dailycaller.com/2014/03/11/improving-the-endangered-species-act-for-the-21st-century/.

20. Tim McClintock, "Stopping Unauthorized Appropriations," June 5, 2013, https://mcclintock.house.gov/newsroom/speeches/stopping-unauthorized-appropriations.

CHAPTER 9: PROFITEERING IN THE SWAMP

1. "Federally Created Entities: An Overview of Key Attributes," United States Government Accountability Office, http://www.gao.gov/assets/300/297944.pdf.

2. Christopher DeMuth Sr. and Michael S. Greve, *Agency Finance in the Age of Executive Government,* George Mason

University Antonin Scalia Law School, June 20, 2016, http://
administrativestate.gmu.edu/wp-content/uploads/2016/03/
DeMuth-Greve-For-Profit-Govt-final.pdf.

3. Associated Press, "Federal boat bought with fishing fines used
    for fun," *HeraldNet*, February 17, 2012, http://www.
    heraldnet.com/news/federal-boat-bought-with-fishing-fines-
    used-for-fun/.

4. Scott P. Brown, "Letter to President Obama,"
    Federalnewsradio.com, April 13, 2012, http://www.
    federalnewsradio.com/wp-content/uploads/pdfs/Brown_
    NOAAletter.pdf.

5. Bore-Head007, "Senator Scott Brown asks President Obama
    for NOAA accountability citing GSA Scandal," *NewsVine*,
    April 18, 2012, http://bore-head007.newsvine.com/_
    news/2012/04/18/11263151-senator-scott-brown-asks-
    president-obama-for-noaa-accountability-citing-gsa-scandal.

6. James Gattuso, "Agricultural Marketing Fees: Not Just for
    Christmas Trees," Daily Signal, November 10, 2011, http://
    dailysignal.com/2011/11/10/agricultural-marketing-fees-not-
    just-for-christmas-trees/.

7. Ibid.

8. Hannah Northey, "Nuclear Waste: U.S. ends fee collections
    with $31B on hand and no disposal option in sight," *E&E
    News*, May 16, 2014, http://www.eenews.net/
    stories/1059999730.

9. Josh Hicks, "How would a shutdown impact Homeland
    Security?" *Washington Post*, September 30, 2013, https://
    www.washingtonpost.com/news/federal-eye/wp/2013/09/30/
    how-would-a-shutdown-impact-homeland-security/.

10. Jason Snead, "Instead of Raiding the Assets Forfeiture Fund, Congress Should Simply Discontinue It," The Heritage Foundation, Issue Brief #4469 on Legal Issues, November 20, 2015, http://www.heritage.org/research/reports/2015/11/instead-of-raiding-the-assets-forfeiture-fund-congress-should-simply-discontinue-it.

11. "Iowa Forfeiture," Institute for Justice, http://ij.org/case/iowa-forfeiture/.

12. Melissa Quinn,"Judge Makes Government Pay Legal Fees to Store Owner Whose $107,700 Was Seized by IRS," Daily Signal, February 3, 2016, http://dailysignal.com/2016/02/03/judge-makes-government-pay-legal-fees-to-store-owner-whose-107700-was-seized-by-the-irs/.

13. "Iowa Forfeiture," Institute for Justice.

14. Rosalind S. Helderman, Tom Hamburger, and Steven Rich, "Clintons' foundation has raised nearly $2 billion—and some key questions," *Washington Post*, February 18, 2016, https://www.washingtonpost.com/politics/clintons-raised-nearly-2-billion-for-foundation-since-2001/2015/02/18/b8425d88-a7cd-11e4-a7c2-03d37af98440_story.html?tid=a_inl.

15. Matthew Mosk, Brian Ross, and Brian Epstein, "'FOBs': How Hillary's State Dept. Gave Special Attention to 'Friends of Bill' After Haiti Quake," ABC News, October 11, 2016, http://abcnews.go.com/Politics/fobs-hillarys-state-dept-gave-special-attention-friends/story?id=42615379.

16. Eric Lichtblau, "Emails Renew Questions About Clinton Foundation and State Dept. Overlap," *New York Times*, August 10, 2016, http://www.nytimes.com/2016/08/10/us/politics/emails-renew-questions-about-clinton-foundation-and-state-dept-overlap.html.

17. Hugh Hewitt, "'Clinton Cash'" Author Peter Schweizer On
     The Latest Clinton Foundation Revelations And His
     Relationship With Trump Campaign CEO Steve Bannon,"
     Hughhewitt.com, August 26, 2016, http://www.hughhewitt.
     com/clinton-cash-author-peter-schweizer-latest-clinton-
     foundation-revelations-relationship-trump-campaign-ceo-
     steve-bannon/.
18. One of the best and most up-to-date summaries is Edward
     Klein's book *Guilty as Sin: Uncovering New Evidence of
     Corruption and How Hillary Clinton and the Democrats
     Derailed the FBI Investigation*, (Washington, DC: Regnery,
     2016).

CHAPTER 10: WHEN WASHINGTON TAKES CONTROL

1.   D. T. Stallings, *A Brief History of the United States
     Department of Education: 1979–2002* (Durham, NC: Center
     for Child and Family Policy, Duke University, 2002), https://
     childandfamilypolicy.duke.edu/pdfs/pubpres/
     BriefHistoryofUS_DOE.pdf.
2.   Joel Klein, "The Failure of American Schools," *The Atlantic*,
     June 2011, http://www.theatlantic.com/magazine/
     archive/2011/06/the-failure-of-american-schools/308497/.
3.   Cristina Marcos, "House narrowly votes to renew No Child
     Left Behind after drama," *The Hill*, July 8, 2015, http://
     thehill.com/blogs/floor-action/house/247297-house-votes-to-
     renew-no-child-left-behind.
4.   Peter F. Drucker, *The Effective Executive*, revised ed. (New
     York: Harper Business, 2006), 108.

5.   Michael Sargent, "Going Nowhere Fast: Highway Bill
     Exacerbates Major Transportation Funding Problems," The
     Heritage Foundation, Issue Brief #4494 on Transportation,
     Budget and Spending, December 3, 2015, http://www.
     heritage.org/research/reports/2015/12/going-nowhere-fast-
     highway-bill-exacerbates-major-transportation-funding-
     problems.

6.   Michael Sargent, "Highway Trust Fund Basics: A Primer on
     Federal Surface Transportation Spending," The Heritage
     Foundation, Backgrounder #3014 on Transportation, May 11,
     2015, http://www.heritage.org/research/reports/2015/05/
     highway-trust-fund-basics-a-primer-on-federal-surface-
     transportation-spending.

7.   Kelly Weill, "Federal act pressures city to remove oversize
     Times Square billboards," *Politico*, May 1, 2015, http://www.
     politico.com/states/new-york/city-hall/story/2015/05/federal-
     act-pressures-city-to-remove-oversize-times-square-
     billboards-088998.

8.   "Obama Administration: Times Square's Iconic Billboards
     Must Be Removed Or Else," CBS New York, May 5, 2015,
     http://newyork.cbslocal.com/2015/05/05/times-square-
     billboards-highway-beautification-act/.

9.   Sargent, "Highway Trust Fund Basics."

10. Michael Sargent, "Highway Trust Fund 'Patch' Uses TSA Fees
     to Fund Roads (Yes, Seriously)," *Daily Signal*, July 15, 2015,
     http://dailysignal.com/2015/07/15/highway-trust-fund-patch-
     uses-tsa-fees-to-fund-roads-yes-seriously/.

11. "Deficient Bridges by State and Highway System," U.S.
     Department of Transportation, Federal Highway

Administration, January 27, 2015, http://www.fhwa.dot.gov/bridge/deficient.cfm.

12. Mead Gruver, "Wyoming study: Fracking likely not behind well water problem," Associated Press, November 10, 2016, http://bigstory.ap.org/article/0466ca821e2f42e59a80d1b5641f696e/wyoming-study-fracking-likely-not-behind-well-water-problem.

13. Jazz Shaw, "'Close the books' on the *fracking contaminates ground water* myth," *Hot Air*, November 12, 2016, http://hotair.com/archives/2016/11/12/close-the-books-on-the-fracking-contaminates-ground-water-myth/.

14. "The Nine Most Terrifying Words," YouTube video, posted by 01101010charles's channel August 6, 2011, https://www.youtube.com/watch?v=xhYJS80MgYA.

15. George F. Will, "'Whatever it Takes,'" *Newsweek*, http://www.newsweek.com/whatever-it-takes-196192.

16. Terence P. Jeffrey, "21,995,000 to 12,329,000: Government Employees Outnumber Manufacturing Employees 1.8 to 1," CNS News, September 8, 2015, http://cnsnews.com/news/article/terence-p-jeffrey/21955000-12329000-government-employees-outnumber-manufacturing.

17. Iain Murray, *Stealing You Blind: How Government Fat Cats Are Getting Rich Off of You*, (Washington, DC: Regnery, 2011).

18. Carol Morello and Ted Mellnik, "Seven of nation's 10 most affluent counties are in Washington region," *Washington Post*, September 19, 2012, https://www.washingtonpost.com/local/seven-of-nations-10-most-affluent-counties-are-in-washington-region/2012/09/19/f580bf30-028b-11e2-8102-ebee9c66e190_story.html.

19. Bill Allison and Sarah Harkins, "Fixed Fortunes: Biggest corporate political interests spend billions, get trillions," Sunlight Foundation, https://sunlightfoundation. com/2014/11/17/fixed-fortunes-biggest-corporate-political-interests-spend-billions-get-trillions/.

20. Maggie Severns, "How Washington created some of the worst schools in America," *Politico*, November 25, 2015, http:// www.politico.com/story/2015/11/how-washington-created-the-worst-schools-in-america-215774.

21. Gregory Korte, "U.S. has 42 programs to help you get to the doctor," *USA Today*, April 13, 2015, http://www.usatoday. com/story/news/politics/2015/04/13/gao-duplication-nation-report-2015/25713359/.

22. Jenni Grubbs, "Log Lane getting many new signs," *The Fort Morgan Times*, March 13, 2016, http://www. fortmorgantimes.com/ci_29634476/log-lane-getting-many-new-signs.

23. Nicholas Pacifico, "Federal Improper Payments are Significant, Costing Taxpayers Billions," Project on Government Oversight, July 12, 2016, http://www.pogo.org/ our-work/reports/2016/introduction-to-improper-payments. html.

24. Mark K. Matthews, "VA warned repeatedly about cost overruns of $1.7 billion Aurora hospital," *The Denver Post*, September 21, 2016, http://www.denverpost.com/2016/09/21/ aurora-va-officials-warned-repeatedly/.

25. Statement of David Wise, director physical infrastructure, "Federal Real Property: Excess and Underutilized Property Is an Ongoing Challenge," United States Government

Accountability Office, April 25, 2013, http://www.gao.gov/
assets/660/654159.pdf.

26. "NISP Overview," Northern Water, http://www.
northernwater.org/WaterProjects/NISP.aspx.

27. Bruce Finley, "Chatfield Reservoir water supply project OK'd
by feds, faces lawsuit," *The Denver Post,* October 9, 2014,
http://www.denverpost.com/2014/10/09/chatfield-reservoir-
water-supply-project-okd-by-feds-faces-lawsuit/.

28. Aaron Bialick, "'Not a Freeway'—Re-branding the Excesses
of the $1.4B Presidio Parkway," *StreetsBlog SF,* September 11,
2014, http://sf.streetsblog.org/2014/09/11/not-a-freeway-re-
branding-the-excesses-of-the-presidio-parkway/.

CHAPTER 11: HOW PRESIDENT TRUMP CAN DRAIN THE SWAMP

1. As quoted by James Madison in *Federalist No. 47.*

2. Kevin Liptak, "Eyeing Trump, Obama takes new action to
ban Arctic drilling," CNN, December 21,2016, http://www.
cnn.com/2016/12/20/politics/arctic-drilling-ban-obama-
trump/.

3. "Executive Order—Planning for Federal Sustainability in the
Next Decade," The White House Office of the Press Secretary,
March 19, 2015, https://www.whitehouse.gov/the-press-
office/2015/03/19/executive-order-planning-federal-
sustainability-next-decade.

4. Rick Ungar, "Here Are The 23 Executive Orders On Gun
Safety Signed Today By The President," *Forbes,* January 16,
2013, http://www.forbes.com/sites/rickungar/2013/01/16/
here-are-the-23-executive-orders-on-gun-safety-signed-today-
by-the-president/#6c69bf5c7cff; "Obama Issues Executive

Actions on Guns," NRA-ILA, January 8, 2016, https://www.nraila.org/articles/20160108/obama-issues-executive-actions-on-guns.

5. Reid Epstein, "Obama signs minimum wage order," *Politico*, February 12, 2014, http://www.politico.com/story/2014/02/miniumum-wage-executive-order-barack-obama-103450.

6. Gardiner Harris, David E. Sanger, and David M. Herszenhorn, "Obama Increases Number of Syrian Refugees for U.S. Resettlement to 10,000." Nytimes.com, September 10, 2015, https://www.nytimes.com/2015/09/11/world/middleeast/obama-directs-administration-to-accept-10000-syrian-refugees.html?_r=0. Accessed January 11, 2017.

7. Glenn Kessler, "How many pages of regulations for 'Obamacare'?" *Washington Post*, May 15, 2013, https://www.washingtonpost.com/blogs/fact-checker/post/how-many-pages-of-regulations-for-obamacare/2013/05/14/61eec914-bcf9-11e2-9b09-1638acc3942e_blog.html?utm_term=.71326ea7fcbf.

8. Patrick McLaughlin, "An Economy Buried by Regulations," *US News*, August 27, 2013, http://www.usnews.com/opinion/blogs/economic-intelligence/2013/08/27/regulations-cost-the-us-economy-trillions-of-dollars.

9. "Donald J. Trump's Five-Point Plan For Ethics Reform," Donald J. Trump website, October 17, 2016, https://www.donaldjtrump.com/press-releases/donald-j.-trumps-five-point-plan-for-ethics-reform.

10. Caitlin Yilek, "Trump: I will eliminate U.S. Debt in 8 Years," *The Hill*, April 2, 2016, http://thehill.com/blogs/ballot-box/presidential-races/275003-trump-i-will-eliminate-us-debt-in-8-years.

11. "RE: Suggested Policy Solutions," Memorandum, Issue One to Hon. Ken Buck. December 19, 2016.

12. For more on this underappreciated fact, see Iain Murray, *Stealing You Blind: How Government Fat Cats Are Getting Rich Off of You* (Washington, DC: Regnery, 2011).

CHAPTER 12: USING THE CONSTITUTION TO DRAIN THE SWAMP

1. Edwin Chen and Michael Ross, "Balanced-Budget Amendment Falls Short in Tight Senate Vote: Congress: Centerpiece of GOP's 'contract with America' is defeated by two-vote margin. Dole threatens to revive measure, possibly during election season," *Los Angeles Times*, March 3, 1995, http://articles.latimes.com/1995-03-03/news/mn-38285_1_balanced-budget-amendment.

2. Steve Daley, "1 Vote Shy, Gop Delays Budget Bill," *Chicago Tribune*, March 1, 1995, http://articles.chicagotribune.com/1995-03-01/news/9503010260_1_amendment-social-security-senate-floor.

3. "NCSL Fiscal Brief: State Balanced Budget Provisions," National Conference of State Legislatures, www.ncsl.org/documents/fiscal/statebalancedbudgetprovisions2010.pdf.

4. Madison, *Federalist* No. 51, 288.

5. Madison, *Federalist* No. 51, 290.

6. William Tyler Page, "The American's Creed," U.S. Constitution, http://www.usconstitution.net/creed.html.

7. Robert C. Cotner, ed., *Theodore Fosters' Minutes of the Convention Held at South Kingston, Rhode Island, in March, 1790* (Providence, Rhode Island: Rhode-Island Historical Society, 1929), 57.

8.   "Excerpts from American Enterprise Institute's Panel
      Discussion on Article V with Panelist Antonin Scalia," May
      23, 1979, Convention of States, http://www.
      conventionofstates.com/justice_antonin_article_v_convention.

CHAPTER 13: THROW THE BUMS OUT—AND OTHER REFORMS

1.   Amy Roberts, "By The Numbers: Longest-serving members of
      Congress," CNN, June 7, 2013, http://www.cnn.
      com/2013/06/07/politics/btn-congressional-tenure/.
2.   Carl Hulse, "As Trump Embraces Term Limits, Allies in
      Congress Pull Away," *New York Times*, November 17, 2016,
      http://www.nytimes.com/2016/11/17/us/politics/as-trump-
      embraces-term-limits-allies-in-congress-pull-away.html?_r=0.
3.   Hill Staff, "McConnell Becomes Longest Serving Ky.
      Senator," *The Hill*, January 12, 2009, http://thehill.com/blogs/
      blog-briefing-room/news/39677-mcconnell-becomes-longest-
      serving-ky-senator.
4.   James Madison, *Notes of Debates in the Federal Convention
      of 1787* (Athens: Ohio University Press, 1985), 371.
5.   Kevin McCarthy, "2016 House Calendar," https://www.
      majorityleader.gov/wp-content/uploads/2011/07/2016-
      MONTHLY-CALENDAR.pdf.
6.   Ryan Grim and Sabrina Siddiqui, "Call Time for Congress
      Shows How Fundraising Dominates Bleak Work Life,"
      Huffington Post, January 8, 2013, http://www.
      huffingtonpost.com/2013/01/08/call-time-congressional-
      fundraising_n_2427291.html.

7.   Tom McClintock, "Stopping Unauthorized Appropriations," Speeches, June 5, 2013, https://mcclintock.house.gov/ newsroom/speeches/stopping-unauthorized-appropriations.

8.   Phil Kerpen, "Kerpen: End Unauthorized Federal Spending," Conservative Review, March 29, 2016, https://www. conservativereview.com/commentary/2016/03/end- unauthorized-federal-spending.

9.   *Field v. Clark*, 143 U.S. 649, 692 (1982).

10. Ben Weyl, Seung Min Kim, and Burgess Everett, "Senate advances budget deal that doesn't exist yet," *Politico*, September 20, 2016, http://www.politico.com/story/2016/09/ senate-budget-deal-campaign-finance-internet-228428.

CHAPTER 14: WHAT YOU CAN DO TO DRAIN THE SWAMP

1.   Cynthia Lummis, wife of Al Wiederspahn, in a personal interview with Bill Blankschaen. Atlanta, Georgia, September 1, 2016.

2.   Megan McArdle, "The New Louisiana Purchase: Obamacare's $4.3 Billion Boondoggle," *The Atlantic*, March 6, 2012, http://www.theatlantic.com/business/ archive/2012/03/the-new-louisiana-purchase-obamacares-43- billion-boondoggle/254003/.

3.   "James Madison, Virginia Ratifying Convention," The Founders' Constitution, University of Chicago Press and Liberty Fund, http://press-pubs.uchicago.edu/founders/ documents/v1ch13s36.html.

4.   "Ronald Reagan Quotes," BrainyQuote, https://www. brainyquote.com/quotes/authors/r/ronald_reagan.html.

INDEX

W

Y